TRUMPING TRUMP?

A JANUARY Prelude to the 2018 Mid-Term Election Campaign

By

Dr. Roger Hite

Other Titles by Roger Hite

A Tale of Two Cultures: The End of the First Year of
Trump's Era (2018)
Mr. Trump Goes to Washington: The first 100 days
(2017)
Trumping up the Establishment (2017)
Christmas Blessings! Faith and the Human Trinity
(2016)
Eulogies (2016)
The Reluctant Coronation (2016)
Operation Double Down (2016)
Trumping the Queen (2016)
Poetry Trumps Prose (2016)
Ditch Santa! (2015)
Growing Old: The Best Is Yet to Be (2015)
America, Going to Hell in A Handbasket: A Boomer's
Political Lament (2015)
Presidential Voices of My Time (2015)
A Blessed Duck! (2015)
The Shoe-Box Miracle (2015)
Mission before Margin (2015)
Beautiful Lies (2015)
Re-Wrapping Christmas (2014)
Crappy Medicine (2014)
The Green Sash Mentors (2014)
Separation of Church and State (2014)
But for the Grace of God (2014)
Relishing Two Decades of Spring (2014)
A Stack of Newspapers (2014)
The Inheritance (2013
A Gospel of Organizational Leadership (2013)
My Life's Work (2013)
My Media Nanny (2013)
Still Kicking! (2013)

The Mule-Kicker's Dialogues (2013)
Roger's Run (2012)
Bonnie's Time (2012)
The Great Health Care Decision (2012)
Dog-Mom (2011)
The Nun of Camelot (2011)
From Groundhog Day to Camelot (2010)
I Still Buy Green Bananas (2010)
The Return to Marlboro (2010)
Unwrapping Christmas (2009)
Last Stop before Paradise (2009)
Buster's View (2009)
The Loser (2008)
Buster's Spirit (2008)
The Iron Butterfly (2008)
Nesting Among Ducks (2008)
Cottage by the Sea (2007)
The Foul Game (2007)
Vivid Imagination (2005)
The Sister Deal (2004)
The God Switch (2004)
Soul Merchants (2004)
Buster's View (2002)
Mirror Man (2001)
The Twelve Candle Miracle (1999)
What's the Good Word? (1999)
The Ebony Snowflake (1999)
The Art of Awe (1998)
Our Gift (1998)
Buster at My Side (1997)
Buster at the Gate (1995)
Buster at the Wall (1994)

Dedication

To my *Professor Emeritus* friend
Dr. Norman Page,
A Liberal Democrat rooting for a 2018 early
political Christmas present in November!

Preface

Saturday, December 30, 2017

Is 2018 destined to be the political year—as some anti-Trump pundits predict—when Democrats finally "trump" Trump? Will it be a prelude to their fondest dream of a 2020 Presidential campaign in which the "Dump Trump" rhetoric becomes reality?

Will this New Year prove to be an end to the Democratic Party's year-long "winter of discontent" and give rise to a glorious sunrise of a new, reinvigorated Democratic political agenda?

If history is any indicator, it could be foreshadowing demise for Republicans as surely as former sports commentator—the colorful Don Meredith—used to start singing to his broadcasting-booth partner in his twangy voice whenever he felt the outcome of a Monday-night football game was inevitable: *"Turn out the Lights, the party's over!"*

The Washington Post journalist Daniel J. Balz could not wait to hear the first chorus of Meredith's song. He didn't want to be preempted by fellow reporters anxious to write the first piece of political punditry for the year 2018.

Instead, he launched his political fireworks display of predictions on the day before New Year's Eve. It was a "cautiously optimistic" dip into what promises to be troubled waters for the republican majorities in both congressional chambers.

Balz's story was published under the headline: *"Democrats think 2018 will be a good year, but are they realistic about their own problems?"*

The article seemed like a perfect place to begin this January prelude to the 2018 mid-term elections. It underscores a host of conventional wisdom shared by Democratic followers. Donald Trump's administration is characterized as the party of the rich—and the Democrats are banking on a tsunami of democratic voter turnout that puts at least the House control back in the hands of democrats.

It is an ambitious task to "trump" Trump's GOP base in the mid-term elections. Here are some of the facts:
- Democrats need to gain 24 seats to take control of the House

- In the Senate they only need a net of two seats to gain control
- In the Senate there are far more democratic seats at risk, however, compared with vulnerable republican seats

Balz's article cites an analysis done by the highly respected Cook Political Report. It lists 17 Republican House seats as toss-ups and one leaning to the Democrats. Another 22 GOP seats are in the "lean-Republican" category—meaning they are at risk this year in the upcoming election. In contrast, Cook list just four Democratic seats as toss-ups and five as "lean-Democrat."

Even though Balz reflects optimism, he is also cautious:

"Many current indicators point to rough days ahead for the Republicans, unless passage of the tax bill somehow changes their fortunes. From the president's low approval ratings to the high energy among rank-and-file Democrats, as well as recent polls showing that the public prefers Democratic candidates for the House by a sizable margin, there is ample evidence that the GOP faces a typically bad midterm election, or possibly worse. One caveat to all that: In the era of Trump, nothing should be taken for granted in terms of traditional metrics."

Balz cautions the Democratic Party, however, to get beyond the Resist-Trump campaign rhetoric. He encourages Democrats to move their party from the aging establishment political figures to a younger image.

For example, in the House, the top three Democratic leaders are in their late 70s. In the Senate, the two top leaders are in their late 60s or early 70s.

He points out that among the party's prospective presidential candidates, Sanders is 76, former Vice President Joe Biden is 75, and Senator Elizabeth Warren is 68.

Howard Dean, former governor of Vermont and former chair of the Democratic National Committee, is among those calling for a search for youth. He argues younger Americans—under 35—are an important Democratic constituency. He wants his party to find a presidential candidate who "turns on" this younger voter cohort.

Will the Republicans fail to raise the party's image among voters and relinquish the House to the Democratic Party?

Or, will the Democratic Party falter and fail to capitalize on the opportunity to rebuild their party and articulate a "middle-class" champion image to their aging political party?

Buckle-up and get prepared for one of the most contentions mid-term election campaign in recent American history.

Will the Democratic Party be able to "trump Trump?"

The purpose of this book is to chronicle on a month-by-month, day-by-day basis the events leading up to the November 2018 Mid-Term Congressional elections and to speculate on what the election foreshadows for the 2020 Presidential contest.

This is the first month assessment of how Democrats and Republicans are setting the political tactics and strategies to make their party's best case in the upcoming election. See who is emerging in the Democratic Party as its 2020 leader.

Welcome to JANUARY! Stay tuned to see which Democratic wannabe presidential candidate muscles to the front of the pack for 2020. See how much Congressional power of the GOP is eroded for 2018.

1

"Happy New Year!"

Monday, January 1, 2018

President Trump rang in the New Year with a traditional gala event ending his 10-day holiday vacation at his Mar-A-Lago estate in Florida.

The holidays were punctuated by a great victory on the tax-reform bill President Trump signed into law before he and the rest of Congress adjourned for the Christmas season. Although the law was characterized by democrats as a lump of coal in middle-class Christmas stockings and a gold brick in the stockings of the rich, Trump had every reason to see the successful legislation a great big present under his leadership Christmas tree.

And, by the way, the President enjoyed many days playing golf on one of his famous courses—and using the leisure time interspersed with domestic and foreign political issues.

Sandwiched between golf games and hosting events with members of his exclusive golf club, Trump did find time to immerse himself in his favorite social media. He tweeted out a year-end message:

"Friends, supporters, enemies, haters, and even the very dishonest Fake News Media, a Happy and Healthy New Year."

The New Year's Eve dinner was a four-course meal consisting of an iceberg wedge salad with Roquefort dressing, Maine lobster, pan-seared sea bass and sliced tenderloin, and baked Alaska for dessert—underscoring the President's seems unconcerned about maintaining a "heart healthy" diet. [Keep this menu in mind later in the month when the President undergoes his annual physical exam.]

* * * * * * * *

The Washington Post reporters Sean McElwee and Joh Green didn't waste time setting the political table for the 2020 Presidential election.

Their article set out the case that Democratic Senator from New York, Kirsten Gillibrand, as an aspiring candidate trying to get off to an early start in positioning herself for the 2020 challenger to Donald Trump.

They make the argument she is quietly amassing an anti-Trump voting record in the Senate unrivaled by her fellow Democratic colleagues in the Senate. They infer such activity signals her early campaign strategy. McElwee and Green write:

"Over her nine years in the Senate, she has had a reasonably liberal voting record. But she has been especially anti-Trump over the past year. . .

For most Democrat senators, you can get a good idea of how often they'll vote for Trump's agenda by looking at their career voting record or Trump's performance in their state. But for Gillibrand these relationships only partly explain her anti-Trump stance during Trump's first year in office. We need some other factor to explain her particularly anti-Trump stance—like positioning herself to be the Democrats' presidential nominee in 2020, running to the left."

Of course, this outspoken liberal democrat from New York is the woman who took Hillary Clinton's senate seat. With the recent flap about sexual harassment in the workplace scandalizing several men in Congress, Gillibrand has gone on record saying she wished she had been more outspoken at that time and insisted on calling for Bill Clinton to resign after the Lewinsky scandal. Even though she was a Hillary supporter in the 2016 campaign, her comments obviously didn't settle well with the Clinton political machine.

We may not be too long into the New Year until the main stream media begins beating the bushes of the Democratic current vast wasteland of "resist Trump" politicians eager to inherit the mantel of leadership for the 2020 Presidential election.

If you're keeping score, put a GPS tracker on Gillibrand and discover where she travels in support of democratic candidates in the upcoming months. Will she starts rivalling the resurrected political aspirations of former VP Joe Biden?

2

"Predicting Political Player 'Draft' for 2020"

Tuesday, January 2, 2018

Georgia and Alabama football teams emerged yesterday as the all-SEC Conference final contenders for the national collegiate football championship trophy that will awarded after the game next Monday January 8, 2018. President Trump promises he will be present at the game in the Mercedes-Benz facility in Atlanta, Georgia.

It is a good thing the Trump administration has at least temporarily stimulated the economy and passed a tax cut for 80% of the American families.

The avid football fanatic, however, is going to have to spend the average annual tax-cut for a family of four on a single ticket! Unless, of course they bought 4 tickets before knowing who the participants would be for the championship contest—in which case they would only spend half of their projected tax-cut savings!

Given the game is being played between SEC teams in Georgia, however, prices of tickets have sky rocketed. The cheapest ticket now available on Stub Hub is $1,950. The most expensive are suite tickets going at $90,000 dollars. A 50-yard line ticket is going for $13,275. [Keep in mind the cheapest face-value ticket price for the game is $285 dollars.]

The betting odds give Alabama a 4-point advantage over Georgia.

* * * * * * *

Football predictions and odds-makers have been a lot more accurate these days than presidential election polls. That doesn't stop the political pundits, however, from engaging in making predictions.

Like early speculations on next year's football rankings even before the current season ends, presidential politics contest seems to have no seasonal boundaries as witnessed by the mainstream media eagerness to begin speculation of who is vying for their party's "candidate draft" in the upcoming 2020 Presidential contest.

Today the **NBC News** internet page published an article under the headline *"Democrats Are Already Campaigning for 2020."* Following the pathway of NFL sports pundits, even before one political season ends, it is newsworthy to begin speculating about who is going to go high in the upcoming candidate "draft."

NBC pundits begin their draft speculation by opening their article with the observation:

"Former Vice President Joe Biden is going to look a lot like a presidential candidate this year."

Such a premature conclusion is based on the knowledge Biden is scheduled to travel the nation in 2018 supporting democratic candidates in areas where it is likely his efforts might swing contested mid-term seats in states where Hillary won in 2016. It is a two-fold mission: 1) win enough seats to give democrats the majority in the House; and, 2) highlight the image of Biden as a viable presidential candidate in the eyes of voters and, most important, in the eyes of donors.

The article enumerates there are *"roughly two dozen Democrats who are considering a bid for the White House in 2020."*

Aside from suggesting Biden may be the early front runner, several other possible Senator candidates are identified. Including, Bernie Sanders of Vermont, Kirsten Gillibrand of New York, Kamala Harris of California, Cory Booker of New Jersey, and Elizabeth Warren of Massachusetts, Sherrod Brown of Ohio, and Tim Kaine of Virginia are listed as possible contenders.

Included in the non-congressional leadership column of the potential party "draft" are several mayors: Eric Garcetti of Los Angeles, Mitch Mandrieu of Louisiana, and Pete Buttigieg of South Bend Indiana.

The article also speculates New York Mayor Bill De Blasio, former Virginia Governor Terry McAuliffe, and New York Governor Andrew Cuomo and Montana Governor Steve Bullock may also be contenders.

Unless something extraordinary happens in the Republican primary contest, the article concludes that anyone who tries to upend Trump's nomination by the GOP is *running on a fool's errand.*

Of course, the article had to at least give lip service to potential Republican candidates. The story concludes with this speculation:

"There's been a lot of chatter in political circles about Trump facing a challenger—perhaps Ohio

Governor John Kasich, former Massachusetts Governor Mitt Romney, Senator Ben Sasse of Nebraska or retiring Senator Jeff Flake of Arizona, a vocal critic of the president, Dallas Mavericks owner Mark Cuban, who campaigned for Clinton in 2016, has said that if he runs for president, he will probably do so as a Republican."

The silver-lining for the Trump administration is the possibility all this speculation about candidates will significantly divert media focus from negative attacks on Trump and claims of "conspiracy" and "collusion" with Russia and focus on positive stories about potential Democratic presidential campaign challengers!

But, then again, until a real democratic contender emerges, it may just be more of the same old rhetoric of "Resist Trump!"

Maybe there will be a fake news story revealing billionaire Trump used some of his huge personal rich person's tax-cut windfall to buy a huge blocks of football championship tickets at their face value of $285 dollars—and, through a Russian conspiracy connection with Stub Hub—made another small fortune!

Is ticket scalping an impeachable crime?

3

"Bashing Bannon"

Wednesday, Jan. 3, 2018

President Trump once again reinforced his position as a political counter-puncher. This morning when news of hostile remarks toward him and his family by former political strategist Steve Bannion surfaced in an advanced copy of a book by Michael Wolff, Trump went to his twitter account and tweeted:

"Steve Bannon has nothing to do with my Presidency. When he was fired he not only lost his job, but he lost his mind. Steve was a staffer who worked for me after I had already won the nomination by defeating seventeen candidates, often described as the most talented field ever assembled in the Republican party."

In preview copies of the book now circulating in Washington D.C., Bannon is quoted accusing Donald Trump Junior as committing "Treason" for meeting with Russian representatives and soliciting alleged campaign dirt against Hillary Clinton.

Trump was allegedly outraged by an earlier interview Bannon did with **Vanity Fair** magazine in which he mocked the president's intellect, criticized White House operations and ripped Trump's son-in-law, Jared Kushner and his oldest son, Donald Trump Jr.

In another tweet Trump continued criticism of Bannon:

"Now that he is on his own, Steve is learning that winning isn't as easy as I make it look. Steve had very little to do with our historic victory, which was delivered by the forgotten men and women of this country. Yet Steve had everything to do with the loss of a Senate seat in Alabama held for more than thirty years by Republicans. Steve doesn't represent my base—he's only in it for himself."

Not surprising, the main topic of the White House daily press corps briefing by Press Secretary Sarah Huckabee Sanders was fielding questions regarding the Trump rift with Bannon. She told the press reporters the quotes by Bannon in the book that discredited other staffers in the White House were false and already people who were quoted by Bannon have disclaimed they ever made such remarks.

Trump Republican colleagues in Congress are pleased with this break between Trump and his former strategy adviser because many wanted Trump to disassociate himself with the alt-Right ultra-conservative Steve Bannon.

It didn't take Trump's eldest son too much time to chime in on the Twitter rhetoric against Steve Bannon. In support of his dad, Donald Trump, Jr. sent a tweet to Bannon mocking Bannon for his work in helping the Republicans lose the Alabama Senate Seat to a Democratic candidate, Doug Jones.

Trump son wrote: *"Thanks Steve. Keep up the great work!"*

He later tweeted former White House Communications Director Anthony Scaramucci, who served in the White House for less than two weeks for issuing an interview with the **New Yorker** magazine in which he made a vulgar criticism of Bannon. In his tweet to Scaramucci, he simply said Scaramucci *"pretty much nailed it"* with his vulgar characterization of Bannon.

As one reporter joked with Sarah Sanders in the press briefing, *"I guess this means Bannon won't be on the White House guest list in the future!"*

* * * * * *

After fielding a dozen or more Bannon question, Sanders had to address the volatile tweet Trump made in response to the combative nuclear threat rhetoric issued by North Korea's leader Trump has labeled "Rocket Man."

Essentially, in response to Kim Jong-un's boast he now had a "nuclear button" on his desk, Trump retorted he also has a button, it is bigger, and his nuclear weapon system is larger, and it works.

Many of Trump's critics saw the tweet as a childish and foolish response. Some of the press corps questioned how Trump could be so confrontational with someone the U.S. considers an "unstable and irrational" leader—wondering if it was wise to taunt such an individual. They also questioned whether such tweeting would settle well with our allies in the area interested in avoiding nuclear war with North Korea.

Sanders did her best to deflect such criticism of the President by simply vectoring away from the issue and declaring Trump was "not backing down" or appearing to ignore threats against the United States.

4

"Competency Questioned?"

Thursday, Jan. 4, 2018

Even though much of the country—especially the East Coast where thousands of air flights have been cancelled—is caught in a frigid cold front labeled a "bomb cyclone" because it exhibits high winds, snow, and extreme cold, the political temperature is heating up in Washington, D.C. and the stock market is literally "on fire!"

Today the Dow Jones index for the Stock Market exceeded 25,000 for the first time ever. It also marked the 74 time since the Trump presidency began that the market reached a record increase.

It was, coincidentally, the same day **The Hill** news source published an article by staff writer Brett Samuels under the headline: *"Lawmakers briefed by Yale psychiatrist on Trump's mental health: report."*

At the same time the controversial comedian co-hostess of **ABC's The View** television magazine, Joy Behar, ripped into Trump's mental health by giving one of her "hate Trump" tirades in which she said: *"Trump needs to be medicated and hospitalized."* Her remarks were in response to Trump's recent tweets about the U.S. having a bigger and more powerful nuclear button on his desk, and that his button works! The women on **The View** agreed with Behar's charge that *"Trump would start nuclear war to keep his 'stupid sons' out of jail."*

Whether one likes or abhors Trump, the American public should be anxious about the left-leaning mainstream media raising the issue about mental health and fitness for leadership of the president. It represents still another front on the political battlefield where a war is being waged to undermine Trump's presidency.

Samuels article is a good example of "weaponizing" use of psychiatry to assess the fitness of any political figure.

The news story was not "new" but a rehash of a story published in another left-leaning source, **Politico.** Samuels reports that on Dec 5 and Dec 6 a Yale University psychiatry professor met with a dozen Democratic legislators to discuss the mental fitness of the president.

In his meeting Dr. Lee allegedly reviewed a paper titled, "The Dangerous Case of Donald Trump." It was a collection of testimonials from more than two dozen psychiatric experts in which the group concluded last October: *"We feel that the rush of tweeting is an indication of his falling apart under stress. Trump is going to get worse and will become uncontainable with the pressures of the presidency."*

Even today in the White House press corps briefing, the Press Secretary, Sarah Huckabee Sanders had to deal with questions about the president's mental health—as one reporter pressed the issue as to whether the upcoming annual physical scheduled for the President next week goes beyond assessing his physical fitness, but also involved his mental fitness? Sanders deftly vectored the question by indicating the examination would be done and a traditional medical report will be available.

Some of the political pundits are pointing to this ongoing democratic strategy as a continuation of the effort to use the 25th amendment language to set the stage for a never used process of having the vice president and a majority of the Cabinet declare the president *"unable to discharge the powers and duties of his office"* and remove him.

It is a sad state of political affairs when one party resorts to the tactic of attacking the mental health status of a person not liked and using the expert opinions of a psychiatrist to warrant the conclusion.

It should be noted the Yale University psychiatrist and his colleagues who opined on the mental health of the president are all guilty of violating the professional ethical code prohibiting a psychiatrist from asserting conclusions about anyone mental health without first giving them a personal examination.

Imagine the political chaos we would have if anyone who dislikes an opponent could talk with a psychiatrist and get them to render a professional opinion of the opponent's mental health.

* * * * * * * * *

The climate of Washington D.C. politics was elevated significantly by the tabloidesque new book by Michael Wolff, **Fire and Fury: Inside the Trump White House.** Trump's private attorneys have initiated legal steps to put pressure on the publisher to not circulate the book because it is allegedly fraught with liable and inaccurate facts. Some of the people quoted in the book have indicated non-truthful statements have been attributed to them.

The book's author attributes several harsh criticisms of the Trump White House and Trump's family to statements made by former White House advisor, Steve Bannon. During her press briefing today Sarah Sanders didn't mince words and attacked the book as fraught with lies and inaccuracies.

She told the press corps the words she would use personally to characterize the book was "complete fantasy," "sad," and "pathetic." Regarding the claims the book made about Trump's mental fitness, she said:

"It's disgraceful and laughable. If he was unfit, he probably wouldn't be sitting there, wouldn't have defeated the most qualified group of candidates the Republican Party has ever seen. He is an 'incredible leader.'"

It was rumored Trump sent a cease-and-desist letter to Bannon, indicating he was in breach of his non-disclosure agreement he signed as a former member of the White House Staff. It was also rumored he sent a similar cease-and-desist letter to the book's publisher, Henry Holt & Company requesting they not publish the book and apologize to the President.

When asked by several members of the press corps to explain Trump's motives and verify the cease-and-desist letters, she told reporters they should contact Trump's attorneys regarding the steps—if any—Trump is taking against the author. She clarified Trump's actions were not an example of "prior restraint" on the author's free speech rights by the White House, but an example of Donald Trump's personal rights to challenge in a court of law personally liable statements made against him.

5

"Presidential '*Fake News*'"

Friday, January 5, 2018

Sometimes it takes a serendipitous event to put things in proper perspective. A case in point occurred this evening when my wife and her mother visiting us in Eugene decided to watch an old movie. I agreed to let them select the film from the list available on our pay for view channel.

What did they choose? A film made in 1941 titled *"Nine Lives Are Not Enough."* Who was starring in the film? A young actor named Ronald Reagan!

I was going to go upstairs and watch the basketball game between Oregon and Oregon State but wanted to view the first part of the film. I wanted to get a glimpse of the actor turned politician who became a well-respected two-term President of the United States.

It turned out I got hooked on the b-grade film, not because Reagan was a captivating, talented actor, but because of the irony the film represented in the modern day presidential context.

What was the irony in the plot that seemed relevant to today's politics? Reagan played a young ambitious newspaper reporter who had a history of running down "scoops" on headline news stories. The only problem was he was often wrong and got his newspaper publisher in lawsuits and having to print embarrassing story retractions.

As the story unfolds, Reagan is given a reprimand and demoted from headline story reporter to having to ride along with a couple of officers who deal with mundane stories worthy of back page filler stories.

Reagan, however, uncovers the story of a millionaire commodities trader found dead in a cheap boarding house under unusual circumstances. Reagan follows his intuition and concludes it is a not the suicide it appears to be. He once again convinces his editor to run the story as though it were a murder story. Unfortunately, the investigation jury panel concludes the evidence supports the theory it is a suicide, not a murder.

As far as the editor was concerned, the "fake news" story warranted firing Reagan. Undaunted, Reagan befriends the attractive daughter of the millionaire and convinces her to cooperate with him to find the murderer. The film ends with Reagan finding the murder and the wealthy heir of the murdered millionaire buys the newspaper and allows Reagan to get the last laugh by becoming the head of the newspaper!

It is safe to say nowhere in his wildest imagination could former President Ronald Reagan have ever imagined this role he played in his acting career would foreshadow the story of a future president—Donald J. Trump—and the battle he would wage with Trump-Hating reporters and their daily activities of generating "fake news."

After viewing the film, it was difficult to not continue reflecting on the relationship to Reagan's early acting career and his unlikely rise to prominence in American Presidential history, and the current circumstances of another non-politician who was also elected to the highest office in our government.

The great irony continued to echo in how the public most often compares current President Trump with Ronald Reagan. How curious that in this film, the popular Reagan was cast as the very type of character Trump is so annoyed with in his modern Presidential circumstances. The only major difference is that in the film Reagan isn't deliberately creating "fake news" but is simply jumping the gun and not checking his facts.

The ongoing battle being waged between President Trump and the media is his criticism that the media is deliberately trying to slant and bias the news to undermine his leadership—and often to deliberately create fake news stories masquerading as true news.

How coincidental the news media is currently abuzz with stories emanating from a book written by a so-called journalist, Michael Wolff, under the tile of **Fire and Fury: Inside the Trump White House.**

Wolff's book underscores the new tactical focus of the left-wing news media. The tactic is to now shift the crusade against Trump away from the apparent futile effort to implicate him with Russian collusion, and to focus on his incompetence to lead America.

In an interview Wolff made with BBC radio, he told the book reviewer, *"I think one of the interesting effects of the book so far is a very clear emperor-has-no-clothes effect."*

According to a story published by **Reuters,** Wolff told the BBC interviewer:

"Suddenly everywhere people are going 'oh my God, it's true, he has no clothes.' That's the

background to the perception and the understanding that will finally end this presidency."

The Wolff book is the most recent example of what Trump and his supporters call "fake news."

Trump has not minced his words regarding his opinion of Wolff and the book. He not only disavows he gave any interview to Wolff, as claimed in the book, but takes on his former White House advisor, Steve Bannon who says vicious things about Trump in the book:

"Michel Wolff is a total loser who made up stories in order to sell this really boring and untruthful book. He used Sloppy Steve Bannon, who cried when he got fired and begged for his job. Now Sloppy Steve has been dumped like a dog by almost everyone. Too bad.!"

Punch and counter-punch! There is nothing "fake" about the rhetorical fist-fight Trump is waging with this person he perceives as a purveyor of "fake news."

And, as if to underscore his ongoing anger with the fake news media, Trump is alleged to be preparing to issue his annual "fake news" awards in an upcoming press conference!

And, if anybody cares to look at the economy, stupid, things are otherwise going quite well—in spite of what anyone judges as "fake news!"

6

"Republicans Plan 2018 Agenda"

Saturday, June 6, 2018

Today President Trump met with Republican Congressional leaders at Camp David in Maryland to discuss the party's political agenda for 2018.

After the meeting, President Trump held about a 20- minute press conference in which he highlighted the items discussed at the meeting.

One of the top items on the agenda is immigration reform and the related subjects of the border wall and the status of the DACA immigrants. Trump told the press after the meeting:

"We all want DACA to happen, but we also want great security for our country"

Trump appears to be adamant in his insistence the wall between Mexico and the U.S. in non-negotiable in the discussions about illegal immigration. He still insists that even though he wants 18 billion from Congress for the wall,

Mexico will eventually, in some form, pay for the wall.

Of course, Mexico insists it will not pay for the wall.

The current budget for the wall asks Congress for the additional 18 billion dollars to add 316 miles of wall and fencing along the border and add 407 improvements in the existing barriers. If the complete plan is funded, then it would create a barrier of more than half of the 2000-mile border between the U.S. and Mexico.

Trump is telling Congress he wants to approve a plan allowing DACA "Dreamer" children permanent status in the US but will only do so if the Congress funds the border wall. Trump did not equivocate on his demands for border wall funding:

"I hope we are going to work out our agreement with the Democrats, but we want the wall. The wall's not going to happen, we're not having DACA."

While he was speaking at the press conference, Trump commented on the status of the on-going special council investigation. He told the reporters:

"Everything I've done is 100 percent proper. That is what I do. I do things properly—just so you understand, there's been no collusion. There's been no crime."

During the press conference, Trump reiterated his party's resolve to stop the flow of drugs into the United States. He also reflected with cautious optimism their might be some resolve to the current escalated tension with North Korea.

President Trump was especially optimistic something good might come out of the talks between South and North Korea regarding participation in the upcoming Olympics being held it South Korea. He told the reporters: *"If something can come out of those talk that would be a great thing."*

7

"Battle of Two Cultures"

Sunday, January 7, 2018

There is a series of signs on the Interstate Highway 5 leading through Northern California up into Oregon. The signs reflected the feelings of rural Californians who say they wanted to cut away from much of urban California and form a new independent state called "The State of Jefferson."

When driving up into Oregon there is a huge sign painted in faded red-white-and blue patriotic colors on the roof of an old barn on the right side of the road as one heads up the hill just before the border town of Hilt. It reads, *"Welcome to the State of Jefferson."*

Decades ago when folks drove south from Oregon into California, the sign at the border read: *"Welcome to California"* it appeared just after a sign from the former Oregon Governor, Tom McCall, thanking folks for visiting and encouraged them to return to their homes in California. The theme reflected Oregon provincialism that wanted California visitors, but not migration into the State from its neighbors in the south. The State wanted California tourism, but after their visit wanted them to return home.

Now there is a different sign some wags have attached to the Welcome to California sign. It reads *"Welcome to an Official Sanctuary State— the home of felons and illegals."*

The prank sign underscores the clash between the liberal left-wing resistance to the right-leaning Trump administration. Once again in American history, there is a serious rift brewing between the federal government and a state's sovereignty.

The political clash is symptomatic of the larger problem facing the Trump administration: How to repair what is characterized as "the Tale of Two Cultures" and how to unify the "Divided States of America.

This time it is not a conservative southern state, but a liberal West Coast state asserting its position of "states-rights."

The current fight between the Trump administration and California is apt to continue to erupt into the most bitter political contest between the White House and a state since George Wallace of Alabama challenged the federal government over segregation laws in the 1960's.

The Trump administration's positions on illegal immigration, off-shore oil drilling in the Pacific Ocean off the California coast, and federal laws challenging the recently enacted California law legalizing pot smoking for recreational purposes are symptomatic of the clash of cultures now dominating American politics.

Anyone looking for evidence President Donald Trump is not pleased with leadership in the heavily blue state of California need to look no further than the fact Trump is the first president since Dwight Eisenhower not to visit California during his first year in office.

Not surprising, when one looks at the political dominance of Democrats in California, every state leader is a Democrat, as is the Governor and both leaders of the State's Senate and Assembly. In Congress, Democrats holds 53 seats; only 14 are occupied by Republicans.

Looking forward to the 2018 election, several of the republican held seats are now vulnerable as a result of announced retirements of GOP congressmen. California could well get the last laugh if it yields up sufficient seats to shift the power in the House.

When the Trump administration passes the recent tax reform bill that seemed to punish "blue" states by limiting the SALT tax deductions from federal income tax filings, California legislation proposed a creative way around the law by making state taxes charitable contributions and therefore under state law, fully deductible.

The greatest friction between California's state government and the federal government stems from the controversy of illegal immigration and the willingness of the State to declare itself a "sanctuary state." Previously, the theme of "sanctuary city" contributed to the unfortunate, tragic death of Kate Steinly because of an accidental shooting done by a multiple-time illegal immigrant the San Francisco police refused to hold and turn over to the federal ICE officers.

The fact a San Francisco jury found the illegal immigrant not-guilty of at least "involuntary manslaughter" but only on a minor violation of being a felon with a gun, further enraged the federal justice department. It appears, however, the feds will get the immigrant when he is released from a California prison in a few months, try him for manslaughter, and if convicted, will deport him after he serves his prison term.

To further their sanctuary city argument, the State Senate Leader led the State Legislature to pass the "The California Values Act." In effect, it declares that the whole state of California is under California law now considered a "Sanctuary State."

The law restricts state authorities from cooperating with federal immigration agents, and places limits on agents entering schools, churches, hospitals or courthouses to detain undocumented immigrants. The law went into effect Jan 1st.

A recent declaration of Democratic Governor Jerry Brown praised the State legislation for making the whole state a "sanctuary state" and caused Thomas Hornan, the federal acting director of Immigration and Customs Enforcement [ICE] to say in a **Fox News** interview:

"They are about to see a lot more special agents and a lot more deportation officers. If the politicians in California doesn't want to protect their communities, then ICE will."

When Hornan also suggested that local politicians who support sanctuary policies should be arrested, the mayor of Sacramento, Darrell Steinberg, went to his Twitter account and tweeted:

"They certainly know where to find me!"

If one has a creative imagination and is old enough to recall the turbulent times of the Civil Rights protests of the 1960's, it should be easy to see Governor Jerry Brown standing on the steps of the Capitol in Sacramento with his arms crossed defying the diminutive figure of the former southern Senator from Alabama —now Attorney General—Jeff Sessions--challenging the "States' rights" of California's liberal governor.

8

"Oops—I Misspoke"

Monday, January 8, 2018

Sometimes there is truthful, vindication of claims against the unpopular President Trump and his administration. It appears a remorseful apology was in fact in order from President Trump's former Chief White House strategist Stephen Bannon.

According to an article published in **The New York Times** by Jeremy Peters, Michael Tackett and Noah Weiland, Mr. Bannon regretted it took him five days to issue a clarification and correction to a statement he made to the author Michael Wolff in the book **"FIRE AND FURY: Inside the Trump White House."**

The article repeated quoted comments Bannon made to the news source, **Axios.** Bannon said he viewed the younger Mr. Trump as *"both a patriot and a good man."* He went on to clarify: *"My* *comments were aimed at Paul Manafort, a seasoned campaign professional with experience and knowledge of how the Russians operate. He should have known they are duplicitous, cunning and not our friends. To reiterate, those comments were not aimed at Don Jr."*

There were several other comments by White House insiders decrying the claims made by author Wolff.

Perhaps the most heated defense came from Stephen Miller, one of Mr. Trump's senior advisors. In an interview with **CNN** commentator Jake Tapper, Miller defended Trump and criticized the Wolff account as "vindictive" and "grotesque."

In his defense of Trump, Miller called the president a "political genius." When the argument got heated to the point Tapper was frustrated, he cut off Miller and told his audience he was wasting his audience's time.

Mike Pompeo, the C.I.A. director was interviewed on a Sunday talk show—**Fox News Sunday**—discredited the Wolff account of Trump's mental state as "pure fantasy." He testified: *I'm with him almost every day. We talk about some of the most serious matters facing America and the world, complex issues. The president is engaged. He* *understands the complexity.   He asks really difficult questions of our team at C.I.A."*

* * * * * * *

Last evening Hollywood hosted its annual Golden Globes award show. Given the fact that the movie industry spawned the issue of sexual harassment in the workplace by highlighting the "casting couch" *'don't ask don't tell'* sexual exploits of aspiring women actress by powerful Hollywood producers, it was not surprising the theme of sexual harassment and gender equality dominated the awards.

One of the interesting political twists that came out of the evening's activities was the seeming emergence of Oprah Winfrey as a potential democratic Presidential contender in 2020.

Based on her thoughtful political speech in acceptance of a special award, it didn't take journalists long to begin the speculation she was an ideal candidate to challenge Donald Trump. Ryan Teague Beckwith wrote an extensive speculation piece for **Time Magazine.** It was published under the headline, *"How Oprah Could Beat Donald Trump at His Own Game in 2020."*

The speculation points to the many similarities between a potential Oprah candidate and the

Donald candidate that won the 2016 election. Here are the "facts" that enable Beckwith to make such a speculation:

- Both are well-known television personalities.
- Both are multi-billionaires
- Both have huge Twitter account followers
- Both are skilled at self-promotion.
- Both have been polled in head-to-head comparison and Winfrey has done well.
- Oprah would be like Trump in the sense she has no prior political experience.
- Oprah would have to enter a crowded democratic field of democratic political contenders.

Beckwith concludes the speculation with this ironic observation:

"Democrats may bemoan Trump's empty-calorie celebrity campaign win, but there's no reason to believe that they couldn't face one of their own."

Imagine an Oprah Winfrey/ Mark Cuban billionaire outsider ticket!

* * * * * * *

Well, as it turned out the football pundits proved better than the political polls—they were half-right! Alabama did win the national collegiate football championship game in an overtime contest. However, they didn't cover the 4-point spread because the outcome was Alabama 26, Georgia 23.

President Trump did arrive at the field in Atlanta and participated in the pre-game activities. Of course, the anti-Trump media singled in on Trump as he stood at attention with his hand across his heart and sang the national anthem. They said he appeared not to know the words of the song as they tried to read his lips. There was no mention of how his fly was unzipped? Somebody missed a great story!

9

"Oprah: A Democratic Political Star is Born?"

Tuesday, January 9, 2018

One would have thought the Golden Globes Award Show was a surrogate for the 2020 Democratic Presidential Nominating Convention given the media-chatter on all channels this morning, afternoon, and evening.

Everybody had an opinion. Is she REALLY "actively considering" a run for the White House or is it a delusion of a political party starved for a candidate with huge public recognition and admiration?

But, not so fast. Even though Oprah is loved by her millions of television fans, an article published by **CNN's** Ryan Struyk reports that a Quinnipiac poll revealed *that "nearly seven in 10 voters* *overall, including a majority of Democratic voters, said in the survey they didn't want Winfrey to run. Only 21%--of less than half of those who have a favorable view of her—wanted her to launch a bid for the White House."*

Oprah's close friend Gayle King told viewers of the **CBS** morning show **"This Morning"** that she thinks her friend is "intrigued" by the idea of running for president in 2020. King said, however, that she doesn't think at this point that Winfrey is *"actually considering it."*

Winfrey's long-time partner, Stedman Graham said he believed she would make a good president. He dodged the questioned deftly by saying Oprah wouldn't be so cavalier as to say "yes" at this early stage of the game, but left it open she could be drafted by saying *"it's up to the people."*

An internet article posted on the website of **BANG Showbiz** quoted the British popular singer known professionally as Seal. He was critical of Oprah's speech. He told the publication Oprah's speech was "sanctimonious" in her denial of the past history of Weinstein's behavior. In the article he appeared to accuse Oprah of knowing about the allegations of her Hollywood producer close friend. Seal wrote: *"Oh, I forgot, that's right. . you've heard the rumors, but you had no idea he was serially assaulting young starry-eyed* *actresses who in turn had no idea what they were getting into. My bad. #SanctimoniousHollywood."*

* * * * * * * *

Trump was well advised when he decided to allow the press to have a lengthy presence in the White House meeting with Congressional leaders from both the House and Senate. It served the purpose of giving the press a rare insight into the give and take debate among leadership.

Some of Trump's critics saw the lengthy press presence in the meeting as a calculated attempt to play down the charges made by Michael Wolff in his "tell all book" about inside the Trump White House. It was designed to show Trump in a favorable leadership role, leading discussion and engaging in thoughtful dialogue with members of both parties.

Regardless of the motives, Trump used the occasion to assert his position about building a "Wall". Critics observed, however, he his rhetoric has permutated away from *"and Mexico will pay for it,"* and the "it" is now called a "wall system" to allow for something other than just a physical continuous barrier on the U.S. Mexican border.

In the meeting Trump told reporters and the two dozen bipartisan lawmakers present he was going to sign whatever bill the group could come up with. He said: *"I think my positions are going to be what the people in this room come up with. . .I am very much reliant upon the people in this room."*

Trump also agreed to break the DACA and immigration reform policy decision into two phases. Critics from the GOP seemed anxious about what appeared to be a capitulation on Trump's part because they felt he was conceding the resolve to DACA and in effect not using the leverage to win more concession from the Democrats on comprehensive immigration reform.

10

"Weary of the 'Nabobs of Negativism'"

Wednesday, January 10, 2018

Former VP Spiro Agnew was a word-smith whose talent was above and beyond most of the "Trump-Hating" mainstream media pundits. Recall Agnew resigned while he was being investigated for income tax evasion. Agnew was replaced by President Nixon's appointment of House Minority Speaker Gerald Ford.

Agnew's most famous phrase was written by WH speech writer, Willian Safire for remarks uttered by the media-hating Agnew on September 11, 1970 at the California Republican State Convention. He gave us the perfect metaphorical imagery for what Trump calls the "fake news" pundits. Recall his famous phrase:

"Nattering nabobs of negativism."

A less famous secondary epithet followed when Agnew continued venting his antipathy toward the hostile media of his time:

"They have formed their own 4-H Club—the hopeless, hysterical, hypochondriacs of history."

Anyone who relies on mainstream liberal media coverage of the Trump-era presidency should keep in mind the hostility of the Nixon-hating media and how it eventually led to the down-fall of another unpopular Republican president.

The "Resist-Trump" media represent the same tactic experienced in the Richard Nixon White House. They not only took down VP Spiro Agnew, but eventually pressured President Nixon to resign his presidency.

It doesn't seem to matter the country is prospering as because of the decisions and policies Trump has championed. It seems irrelevant the stock market has surged, unemployment has hit a two-decade low point, consumer optimism is at an all-time high mark, and companies are bringing money and jobs back from off-shore business and investment alternatives.

Despite this remarkable economic picture, it is virtually impossible to find any news coverage of the Trump administration's economic successes. When he does something that warrants accolades—like the extraordinary transparent bi-partisan meeting with House and Senate representatives yesterday to discuss DACA and immigration, it didn't take long for the mainstream media to put a negative twist on the meeting.

In contrast to the nattering against Trump, it was refreshing for a few moments to listen to all the positive chatter the mainstream media gave to the prospect of recruiting Oprah Winfrey as the Democratic Presidential Hopeful in 2020 election.

Whether she is a serious candidate, or whether she would take up such a challenge, it was at least a refreshing departure for the "nabobs of negativism" to talk about something positive for a change.

One must wonder, however, how disconcerting such a prospect as the outsider non-politician like Winfrey was to folks like former VP Joe Biden, Senator Elizabeth Warren, Senator Corey Booker, Senator Bernie Sanders and the dozen or so wannabe Democratic politicians queueing up for the 2020 bid for the Democratic Party?

Even Trump was positive toward the thought of Winfrey as his opponent. He mentioned to the press that he liked her and was on one of her final television programs when she elected to interview him and his family. He also said he would welcome her as the loyal opposition's candidate. And, it Trump modesty aside, boasted he would beat her. In fact, several of the "nattering nabob" pundits showed earlier clips before Trump ran for president in which he speculated he thought she'd make a good VP if he were to run!

* * * * * * * *

Despite the constant criticism from the "nattering nabobs," Trump continues to perform his Presidential duties and to work to advance his agenda.

During the early morning hours Trump held a phone conversation with South Korean President Moon Jae-in and receive assurance and thanks from Moon Jae-in that the talks with North Korean diplomats took place—the first one in two-years. Trump told the press he was pleased with the event and hoped good things came out of the renewed diplomatic dialogue between North and South Korea.

Later in the day Trump met with the Prime Minister of Norway, Erna Solberg, and hosted her for a lunch meeting at the White House. The two leaders held a joint press conference where each praised the strong relations both countries wished to continue. Solberg did mention she was, contrary to Trump, a supporter of the Paris Climate Accords.

However, much of the praise each leader spoke about were the strong economic and trade bonds between the two countries. Trump praised Norway for the strong economic relationships that allowed Norway to purchase several billions of dollars-worth of U.S. manufactured military jets and equipment. He joked with Norway that currently it was one of the few countries we trade with where the U.S. has a trade surplus! He also praised Norway for its supportive role in NATO and thanked them for committing to make their 2% contribution to NATO funding.

During the joint press conference Trump fielded several questions about domestic issues. He affirmed there would not be a DACA deal unless there was support for building the wall, ending chain migration, and the lottery system for selecting immigrants.

Trump also addressed the issue of whether he was willing to meet with Special Investigator Robert Muller in a face-to-face meeting without any pre-conditions. Even though Trump continues to assert his position he was not involved in any conspiracy or collusion with the Russians, he was unwilling to categorially re-assert his earlier statements and simply used the convenient reply, *"we'll see what happens."*

* * * * * * * *

The immigration question was actively pursued by both bi-partisan committees in the House and Senate because of the Trump meeting yesterday.

Against such a backdrop of immigration policy planning, Congress still must figure out a way to avoid a looming government shut-down unless it either gets agreement on a budget bill; or, unless it once again for the third time kicks the can down the road with a continuing resolution that buys additional time to find some mid-point on key budget difference over military spending and infrastructure improvement domestically.

* * * * * * * *

If I were Oprah I would take a serious look at Washington politics currently happening and ask myself, *"why would a highly-successful billionaire businesswoman give up the latter years of life to endure all the 'nattering nabobs of negativism" who would redirect the venom toward yet another "outsider—even if she is more popular than Trump?*

I would ask myself, am I prepared and qualified to run a campaign against the successes Mr. Trump has racked up in his first year in office?

Whoever emerges as the Democratic hopeful in 2020 they are going to be successful to the degree they espouse policies and positions that are different than Trump's. It will be unfortunate if the tactic is simply more of the "resist-Trump and despise-Trump rhetoric!

11

"Good Fences Make Good Neighbors"

Thursday, January 11, 2018

Do good fences make good neighbors? That is a perspective that seems to be lacking in the current heated debate over building a wall on the border with Mexico and the fate of DACA.

Today a lot of activity occurred when a group of six-bi-partisan Senators worked in earnest to craft a draft immigration policy plan addressing the charter given to Congress by President Trump to come up with a solution to the DACA problem he could sign.

One of the non-negotiables given as a condition of Presidential approval was the funding necessary to complete the construction of a physical border wall between Mexico and America.

Today one of the members of the ad hoc Senate committee, Senator Flake, announced there was agreement in a draft policy that would be circulated among senate colleagues to see if it there was sufficient support to that the proposed bill to the President's desk.

When a version of the bill was discussed by Trump in the Oval Office today, he expressed his exasperation with a dimension of the proposed compromise bill that redistributed some of the lottery immigration passports to Africans, Haitians, and El Salvadorians. His vulgar tongue exclaimed why do we want folks from "shithole" countries instead of countries like Norway? Such language, if true, certainly won't help Trump's public perceptions among his critics.

Trump has apparently softened his campaign rhetoric, however, and is now refers to the Wall as "a wall-system of physical barriers" in necessary areas and increased ICE patrol in areas where a fence makes no sense. Trump also has backed away from the notion that Mexico is going to pay for the wall.

In retrospect, it is unfortunate the belligerent and combative Trump campaign rhetoric didn't initially subscribe to the gentle poetic analysis of insisting that "Good Fences Make Good Neighbors."

Such a philosophy was first examined in 1914 when Robert Frost wrote a poem for a collection entitled **"North of Boston."** Over the years Frost's poem **Mending Wall**, has become one of the most analyzed poems written by the famous American poet.

It is somewhat surprising none of President Trump political speech writers ever touched on the theme questioned in this poem's most famous and controversial line: *"Good fences make good neighbors."*

Imagine how different the controversial debate over a border wall could be if it had been introduced and linked to the theme *"good fences make good neighbors."*

Suppose both neighboring countries subscribed to the poet's neighbor's philosophy and agreed to work together to maintain a border fence—despite differing views of its function or the need for the fence.

Of course, it is equally important that the "Resist Trump" critics haven't alluded to the poem in the rhetoric they construct in opposition to Trump's insistence upon building a wall along the border between Mexico and America. The critics know they don't have a case that Frost uses to question the necessity of the wall. They know that unlike Frost's reason for questioning the need for the wall is different than Trump's. Frost's skepticism is simple: *"He is all pine and I am apple orchard. My apple trees will never get across and eat the cones under his pines."*

The poet's neighbor, however, is staunch in keeping alive his father's philosophy that *"good fences make good neighbors."* How curious the current political divide in our country echoes this age-old belief that one should clearly demark one's territory and separate the sovereignty of a country like the sovereignty of an individual's private property.

Recall the poem accounts for a spring wall mending-time between two neighbors who meet and attend to repairing and building the stone wall between their two pieces of property.

The poet Frost questions his neighbor's insistence on building and maintaining the wall. Frost seems to represent the liberal democratic view of globalization and President Trump subscribes to the wisdom of Frost's neighbor's father: *"Good fences make good neighbors."*

Frost tells his neighbor: *"Spring is the mischief in me, and I wonder If I could put a notion in his head: 'Why do they make good neighbors? Isn't it where there are cows. But here there are no cows. Before I built a wall, I'd ask to know What I was walling, in or walling out, and to whom I was like to give offence. Something there is that doesn't love a wall."*

Of course, Trump see the wall as a necessary barrier to preserve the sovereignty of a nation—not to separate and protect natural resources like pine trees and apple orchards, but people of neighboring countries.

The symbolism of the two neighbors with different views of maintaining the fence dividing their properties. They don't agree on why it is necessary but once a year they come together and repair and rebuild the ancient stone fence.

It isn't about arguing if the fence is necessary, it is about maintaining separate views of the world and co-existing as neighbors.

Maybe we should consider softening the acrimony that divides opinions about the efficacy of a fence or a wall. Maybe we should modify the philosophy considered in Frost's poem. Maybe we should say:

"Good neighbors maintain good fences?"

* * * * * * * *

I didn't take long for the mainstream liberal media and the establishment democrats to start diminishing the possibility of an Oprah for President campaign. A reporter for **The Guardian**, Ben Jacobs, wrote *"a recent RAB Research phone poll conducted between 10 and 11 via an on- line survey showed that 76% of Democratic voters had a somewhat favorable or very favorable opinion of the former vice-president. In contrast, only 67% of Democratic voters felt the same about Winfrey"*

Jacobs concluded his article by pointing out one poll showed in running Against Trump, Winfrey would be more popular than Trump by 10 points.

When the three most prominent democratic hopefuls were matched against Winfrey, Biden was the most popular, winning 26% of the votes in a four-way race. Sanders was at 21%, Winfrey at 20% and Warren at 18%.

So, it should not be surprising we are less than half-way through the first month of this mid-term election year and there is already jockeying to get certain horses into the early rail position.

12

"Divided Country? The Real Shit-Storm!"

Friday, January 12, 2018

"Allegedly" and according to a resist-Trump democratic senator from Illinois, Richard Durbin, Trump included the vulgar word "shithole" in describing the government of the country of Haiti.

Once again, the clashing rhetoric of America's two cultures comes to the forefront. Like so much of the Washington D.C. political swamp, the uproar over President Trump's alleged use of offensive language is vectoring the focus away from the real "shitstorm" brewing in the Divided States of America.

Forget about whether Senator Durbin is posturing politically by feigning moral indignant by disclosing his impression of a closed-door heated debate with the President in the White House.

According to an initial public statement Durbin made to the press, and a written press release he wrote after Trump denied the charge, Durbin said President Trump said things in the DACA [Deferred Action for Childhood Arrivals] follow-up meeting that were "hate-filled, vile and racist."

Trump's response to the Durbin comment was that he used "tough" language, but Trump wrote on Twitter: *The language used by me at the DACA meeting was tough, but this was not the language used. What was really tough was the outlandish proposal made—a big setback for DACA.*"

In a follow-up tweet later in the evening Trump wrote:

"Never said anything derogatory about Haitians other than Haiti is, obviously, a very poor and troubled country. Never said 'take them out.' Made up by Demos. I have a wonderful relationship with Haitians. Probably should record future meeting—unfortunately, no trust!"

In an article written by Anne Gearan in **The Washington Post,"** cited as her source *"according to several people briefed on the meeting."* She also wrote *"The White House did not deny Thursday that Trump used the vulgarity, first* *reported by **The Washington Post** and later confirmed by numerous news outlets."*

In a self-righteous further tweet, the offended Senator Durbin wrote: *"I cannot believe that in the history of the White House, in that Oval Office, any president has ever spoken the words that I personally heard our president speak yesterday."*

[Senator Durbin must not have ever been around Richard Nixon or Lyndon Johnson or read about their cursing and vile language!]

Other Senators in attendance at the meeting did not see the language in the same way as Senator Durbin.

For example, after the flap began, Senators Tom Cotton and David Perdue issued a joint statement:

"We do not recall the president saying these comments specifically but what he did call out was the imbalance in our current immigration system, which does not protect American workers and our national interests.

They went on to disparage the disruption created by Durbin's allegations:

Trump brought everyone to the table this week and listened to both sides. But regrettably, it seems that not everyone is committed to negotiating in good faith."

It didn't take long for the hostile, anti-Trump cable news **CNN** to unleash a story critical of Trump. The **CNN** news anchor, Don Lemon began his evening program with this declaration:

*"This is **CNN** Tonight, I'm Don Lemon. The President of the United States is racist. A lot of us already knew that."*

CNN's Anderson Cooper made a similar statement earlier in the evening on his program. He said:

"Not racial. Not racially charged. Racist. Let's not kid ourselves or dance around it. The sentiment the president expressed today is a racist sentiment."

Cooper went on to eulogize his own observations about the Haiti people based on his several trips to the country:

"Haitians slap your hand hard when they shake it. They look you in the eye., they do not blink. They stand tall. They have dignity. A dignity many in this White House cold learn from. A dignity the president with all his money and power could learn from as well."

Even Hillary Clinton interjected her view into the controversy. After the story appeared, she tweeted:

"The anniversary of the devastating earthquake 8 years ago is a day to remember the tragedy, honor the resilient people of Haiti & affirm America's commitment to helping our neighbors. Instead, we're subjected to Trump's ignorant, racist views of anyone who doesn't look like him.

The "shitstorm" generated by the liberal media about the language Durbin attributed to President Trump was viewed, not surprisingly, by the Trump supporters through a whole different lens.

Interestingly, none of Trump's supporters challenged Durbin's claim Trump used crude language in the meeting. They seemed willing to accept it as part of Trump's vernacular.

For example, on **FOX NEWS**, Jesse Waters, a co-host on **The Five**, pointed out *"this is how the forgotten men and women of America talk at the bar. If you're at a bar, and you're in Wisconsin, and you think they're bringing in a bunch of Haiti people, or El Salvadorians, or people from Niger, this is how people talk. It is graceful, No. Is it polite or delicate? Absolutely not! Is it a little offensive? Of course it is! But you know what? This doesn't move the needle at all. This is who*

Trump is. He doesn't care, he shoots from the hip, and if he has offended some people, fine. There are so many more offensive things that are happening in this world.

Another **FOX NEWS** program host, Tucker Carlson defended the president on his show. He told his viewers. *"He[Trump] said something that almost every single person in America actually agrees with. An awful lot of immigrants come to the United States from other countries that aren't very nice. Those places are dangerous, they're dirty, they're corrupt, and they're poor and that's the main reason those immigrants are trying to come here."*

It doesn't make any difference that regardless of one's view of the alleged remarks, it appears the President wasn't talking about the "people" who inhabit the country but describing the miserable conditions the governments of such countries have created and maintained for the people.

What this entire incident demonstrates, however, is the "deep shit" division America has created in the Washington, D.C. political swamp as we struggle to govern our own domestic "shithole."

One of the political talking heads interviewed recently made an excellent observation in a discussion about America being a "Nation of Immigrants."

His point was that anyone who dismisses attempts to write a cogent immigration policy if they disagree with by saying *"that's not who we are,"* should bear the responsibility to define *"Who are we?"*

Better still, it may be time for the "swamp dwellers" to ask: *"Who do we want to be in the future?"*

Perhaps the answer to such a question will get us closer to understanding the forces dividing this country during the Trump-Era of American politics.

And as if further evidence was needed to support the assertion this political shitstorm is symptomatic of a greater problem in American politics, once again the "resist-Trump" voice of Rep. Al Green [D-TX] said he would again introduce a resolution to begin Impeachment of President Trump. Most pundits believe the efforts are more symbolical and will not gain much traction in the House.

Such a policy reality isn't apt to gain much traction in the House of Representatives. Later this afternoon it was learned two ranking Democrats on the House Judiciary Committee Cedric Richmond

[D-LA] and Jerrod Nadler [D-NY] intend to formally introduce a censure resolution after the Martin Luther King J. Day holiday.

* * * * * * *

As evidence real business is still being conducted by the Trump White House, President Trump did once again—however reluctantly—issued an announcement today that the U.S. is continuing to participate in the Iran nuclear deal. The President is required by the terms of the agreement to certify to congress every 90-days Iran is complying with the terms of the agreement. Such a certification was lobbied heavily with many of our European allies who were pleased with Trump's decision.

13

"Trump Pronounced Physically Healthy"

Saturday, January 13, 2018

Late Friday afternoon, the White House physician examined President Donald Trump at Walter Reed military hospital and declared him in *"excellent health."*

Dr. Ronny Jackson, MD—the same physician who served as the White House doctor under President Barack Obama —issued a statement released by the White House. The summary read as follows:

"The examination went exceptionally well. The President is in excellent health and I look forward to briefing some of the details on Tuesday."

In an article written for **The Associated Press** by Catherine Lucey indicated the examination lasted several hours and measured things like Trump's blood pressure, cholesterol, blood sugar, heart rate and weight. Lucey noted that while the exams are not mandatory, it is customary for presidents to undergo a medical exam regularly and release evidence the president is "fit for duty."

The preliminary news about the exam indicated Trump's blood pressure and cholesterol measurements were in the healthy range—but he is using a cholesterol-lowering statin medication. His EKG, chest X-ray, echocardiogram and blood sugar were in the normal range.

Lucey also reported the 6-foot-3 Trump weighed 236 pounds and his Body Mass index of 29.5 put him in the category of overweight for his height.

The article was critical of Trump's choice of exercise compared with former President Obama's habits of weight lifting, running on a treadmill, and playing basketball. Trump, by contrast plays golf but doesn't walk the course but used a golf cart so he gets minimum cardiovascular exercise.

The article concluded by revealing Trump's dietary habits—which are questionable:

"Trump likes fast food, too, along with well-done steaks, chocolate cake and double scoops of vanilla ice cream. He reportedly downs 12 Diet Cokes a day. In their recent book "Let Trump Be Trump," former top campaign aides Corey

Lewandowski and David Bossie described the four main food groups on Trump's campaign plane as 'McDonald's, Kentucky Fried Chicken, pizza and Diet Coke.'"

* * * * * * * *

The physical health of Donald Trump may be a lot better than the most recent reports about the health of the Republican Party in the upcoming Mid-Term elections.

In an article written by Paul Kane for **The Washington Post,** Kane suggests what was initially viewed as an impossible and preposterous assertion about a Democratic victory is now starting to look like it is possible, if not probable.

One supposed election pundit, Charlie Cook, founder of the Cook Political Report is quoted as asserting: *"Just about any fair-minded assessment of the House would show that Democrats have probably more than a 50-50 chance of taking control of the House."*

While Cook is more pessimistic about a Democrat victory in the Senate because there are more contested seats for Democrats than Republicans—especially in states where Trump won by a large majority, Cook is still willing to hedge his bet by declaring:

"When it comes to Senate races, they almost all break in one direction. According to Jennifer Duffy, Cook's Senate race expert, one party has won at least two-thirds of the toss-up races since 1998. In 2016, Republicans won five of seven races the Cook report rated as toss ups. In 2012, Democrats won nine of 10 toss-ups. Democrats will need a performance similar to 2012 to get over the hump to win the majority, but Cook is beginning to sound like a grisly old baseball scout trying to let management know that he has found a special pitcher."

Another pundit, Nate Silver, founder of Five Thirty-Eight polling service, is more pessimistic about the health of the Democratic Party to win the Senate in 201. Lucey quotes Silver:

"In all, Silver gives Democrats a 35 percent chance of winning the Senate. "It's higher than it probably should be given how favorable the Senate map is for Republicans. But it's still a fairly steep hill to climb."

Maybe it's time President Trump and his Republican playing partners start walking the political course instead of ridding in the luxury of their projected conventional Congressional election map.

14

"AP Reports Fairly"

Sunday, January 14, 2018

In this Trump-era of bias and slanted mainstream left-leaning news stories where over 90% of Trump stories are negative, it is refreshing to find an example of fair news coverage.

It is somewhat ironic that half-way through the month of January, a truly newsworthy event occurred that even Donald Trump wouldn't call "fake news!" Instead, he might call it "fair news." It may signal some refreshing non-biased reporting of the first-year of the Trump-era of American politics.

Two reporters for **The Associated Press,** Calvin Woodward and Jill Colvin, published a story headlined in the Eugene **Register-Guard** newspaper under title: *"Trump's Promises: Tax Cuts, No Wall."*

The article begins with a mild criticism chiding Trump for what they call a "spectacular stretch" when he brags he's done *"more in his first year in office than any other president."*

Unlike other mainstream slanted and biased reporting about Trump-era politics—and there is much to fault and criticize—the **AP** article acknowledges Trump has, in fact, accomplished some major things in his first year.

The article asserts: *"But while he's fallen short on many measures and has a strikingly thin legislative record, Trump has followed through on dozens of his campaign promises, overhauling the country's tax system, changing the U.S. posture abroad and upending the lives of hundreds of thousands of immigrants."*

Before assessing the actual accomplishment of Trump's first year—a useful prelude to the President's upcoming State of the Union Address—they establish the premise of their article with this assertion:

"The upshot? For all his rogue tendencies, Trump has shaped up as a largely conventional Republican president when measured by his promises kept in motion. . .the ledger of actions taken is recognizable to Washington: mainstream

Republican tax cuts, pro-business policies (with exceptions on trade), curbs on environmental regulations and an approach to health care that's been in the GOP playbook for years."

The journalists use the bulk of their article critically examining such topics as: taxes, immigration, energy and environment, America First abroad, infrastructure, veterans, health care, and trade. And, while they are critical of many of Trump's shortcomings, they give him praise for such things as stimulating the economy through long-need tax reform, appointment of a Supreme Court justice, reduction of economy limiting federal rules and regulations, and movement on several areas of his campaign trail promises.

Even **FOX News'** program host, Harris Faulkner, took the time on her program to mention the **AP** article and praised the article for giving some positive perspective on Trump's first year in the White House. The program discussion only took issue with whether it was a compliment or a criticism for the **AP** journalists to say Trump was *"largely a conventional Republican president."*

Sadly, Trump seems to have a knack for putting his foot in his mouth by being "Trump" who speaks his mind, often without regard for protocols or political correctness. His critics seize of every opportunity to use his own words to divert attention away from Trump's accomplishments and focus on his shortcomings.

It is refreshing to see a news article like the recent **AP** story that gets beyond the resist-Trump media bias and report in a balanced way the positive as well as the negative.

15

"Martin Luther King, Jr. Birthday Holiday"

Monday, January 15, 2018

Is the 45 President of the United States of America a racist? Some point with disdain at Donald J. Trump and level such a disgusting charge!

How ironic in the Trump-era of American politics the current President should be defending himself against charges of "racism" and being a "racist" for alleged comments he made about immigrants from certain poor and corrupt governed nations like Haiti.

Here we are celebrating a national holiday honoring the birthday of Civil Rights icon, Martin Luther King, Jr. and on the same day several black leaders in Congress are calling our current president a "racist." For example, the esteemed black Congressman John Lewis, one who marched shoulder-to-shoulder with King during the 1960's, joined with several other black congressmen protesting Trump's alleged recent racist remarks by boycotting the upcoming State of the Union Address.

It was pointed out in today's morning news programs that three years ago Senator Lindsay Graham used foul language when referring to immigrants who wanted to come to the U.S. from certain foreign "hell-holes." His point was almost identical to the sentiment behind Trump's outcry that created such a recent stir. Like Trump, Graham wasn't disparaging the people but the government of countries responsible for conditions that made America a highly desirable alternative.

It should also be pointed out Lindsay Graham who was present at the meeting with Trump has not equivocated on his earlier assertion that Trump used the: "shit-hole" explicative during the meeting as alleged by Democratic senator Durbin.

And, in fairness to the follow-up comments made by the two Republican Senators present at the meeting—Senator Tom Cotton and Senator David Perdue—categorically denied Trump used the words attributed to him by Durbin. On several Sunday Morning political news shows, they both charged Durbin was known for distorting private

White House meetings with inaccurate accounts of what transpired.

The flap about Trump being a "racist" because of the alleged—but disputed—account given by Senator Durbin led several members of the Congressional Black Caucus to issue statements indicating their intent to boycott the upcoming State of the Union Address President Trump is scheduled to make before the joint session of Congress at the end of January. Democratic Congresswoman from California, Maxine Waters, said it was a waste of her time to attend and sit and listen to a "liar" make any speech.

How sad that on the holiday in which America celebrates the achievements of one of its most revered Civil Rights leaders, we are a nation deeply divided on issues of race and racism.

How ironic one of the media reporters most often shouted-out questions of the president is *are you a racist?"*

Trump steadfast response is as one would expect: *"I'm the least racist person you've ever interviewed! That I can tell you!"*

* * * * * * * * *

The big flap that came on the heels of indignation over alleged language faux paus by Trump was the critical error a civil servant in Hawaii made by sending out an incorrect e-mail alert that a ballistic nuclear missile was headed toward Hawaii.

The false alert created pandemonium and widespread fear among Hawaiians. It also took 38 minutes for the error to be corrected.

The mainstream media spin on the Hawaiian false alarm was to be critical of Trump for his failure to sit down with the North Korean leader and find a diplomatic solution to diffuse the current angst about an impending nuclear confrontation.

Trump indicated in a press interview he was glad Hawaii acknowledged its fault and accepted responsibility for fixing its system, so such incidents didn't happen in the future.

Oh, and by the way, the Trump administration is also facing a potential shut-down of the federal government this Friday if there is not an agreement on the budget or a fourth continuing resolution.

The Democrats are holding out and insisting a DACA agreement must be attached to the budget bill.

Trump is insisting the Democrats are the cause of any pending government shut-down.

Many of the pundits are shaking their heads and conceding a continuing resolution is almost inevitable as neither party wants to bear the blame for a federal shut-down.

16

"26,000 Dow Market: 123/68 Presidential BP"

Tuesday, January 16, 2018

The market is up. The President's blood pressure is down. The health of the economy is excellent. And, according to the White House physician, Dr. Ronny Jackson, so is the physical and COGNITIVE health of the President.

The physician reported to the press how the President seems to have the ability to wake up each morning and "reset" his perspective—and needs only four to five hours sleep each night to function effectively in his workplace.

The physician's office is across from the President's office—and the doctor says his frequent contact with the president seldom causes him to see the President exhibit signs of personal stress in the job.

The good news of the President's health didn't settle well with his critics.

And, the good news of the economy was not high on the mainstream new radar screen. Nevertheless, at least **FOX Business News** reported it only took 12 calendar days [7 trading days] to move the Dow Jones Industrial Averages from the historical high mark of 25,000 to above the new mark of 26,000—even though the market backed away from the number before the close of the Tuesday market trading and ended 10 points down.

The economic achievement marked the shortest time for Wall Street to advance one-thousand points in the history of the stock market. The stock-watchers pointed out the market showed a volatility of more than 400 points. Some say this may be a harbinger of a market adjustment soon.

How curious it is the political landscape is not basking in the bright sunshine of the strong economic performance. Instead the horizon is fogged over with petty controversies—not the least of which is the on-going Democratic Party's efforts to discredit and disparage President Donald Trump. Today, however, the excellent report on the President's health was a blow to the "resist-Trump" critics.

President Trump seems oblivious to the criticism, however, as he forges ahead in the post-holiday politics.

In a Senate Judiciary hearing with the Secretary of Homeland Security, Kristjan Nielsen, Senator Lindsay Graham made his best effort to get refocused on what went wrong between the highly promising Tuesday meeting and the follow-up Thursday meeting Trump had with the bi-partisan group of Senator who appeared eager to meet his criteria for fashioning a DACA and immigration reform package.

Graham said when the group of six Senators brought to Trump a proposal they felt met Trump's four conditions, some of Trump's advisors must have changed his mind and caused him to reject the proposal. Critics say the plan was not circulated among the larger group who met with the President, but a watered-down version that did not address the four principles [pillars] Trump charted the whole group to address.

And, of course, Senator Durbin's disclosure that Trump allegedly used foul language in referring to immigrants from Haiti, refocused the whole debate from policy to "disparage the President" instead of "making a policy" on DACA and immigration reform.

Some pundits speculate Durbin's remarks were designed to block Trump from having any kind of success on immigration. Other's argued the Trump framework was ideal because it gave both sides something so there was no winner or loser.

It also seems like the DACA policy is going to be used as leverage to bring federal government shut down to the table—a crisis all want to avoid, and nobody wants to get blamed for causing. Republicans say unless there is a continuing resolution on the budget, the shut-down will jeopardize military funding. Democrats feel they must leverage the DACA approval and not end up conceding what could be viewed by Republicans as a victory on the wall funding, chain migration, and merit-based immigration policy.

* * * * * * * *

In the White House Press Briefing today, Press Secretary Sarah Huckabee Sanders allowed the White House physician to highlight the results of the annual physical he performed on President Trump.

The reporters questioned Dr. Ronny Jackson for almost 60 minutes with a barrage of questions about granular detail of his health. It was the most comprehensive report of any President's health. During the physician's comments it was clear

President Trump is in excellent health.   Not only did he release standard statistics about his blood pressure—which is 123 over 68—and that all his vitals are within norms.   His physician said Mr. Trump's cardiovascular health should be the envy of every reporter in the briefing room. Dr. Jackson did indicate he wanted Mr. Trump to lose 15-20 pounds as he is currently at 236 pounds which is too heavy for his 6-foot 3-inch frame. Dr. Jackson also wants the President to get more exercise.

The President did ask the physician to not only give him a standard physical, but to give him a Montreal cognitive test which demonstrated he got 30 out of 30 for a perfect score.

One of the reporters asked how Trump could display psychological disorders in his public behavior and score so high on the extensive Montreal Cognitive Test?

The well-respected non-political former physician for former Presidents Bush and Obama demonstrated frustration with questions by non-medical people—and even some medical professionals—that render assessments without examining the President. He chided the reporter by saying such claims were "tabloid psychiatry."

Another reporter questioned how Trump could score such high marks in his physical and at the same time consume huge quantities of fast food and two six packs of diet coke each day. The physician said Trump secret was based on "genetics." He added to the assessment how Trump did not consume alcohol or tobacco.

After an exhaustive amount of questions, Dr. Jackson told the press corps, "President Trump is fit for duty."

[NOTE: One of my democratic friends who was unexpectedly hospitalized the time the President's medical report was released sent me an e-mail photo of him lying on a gurney hooked up to monitor equipment. His caption was something to the effect: *"Our shit-hole President is presumably in "excellent health" with his junk food diet—and look at me right now."*

Of course, my friend was in remarkably good health before his incident and was discharged from the hospital after a couple of days of tests. The photo showed my friend smiling and in good spirits but scratching his head about the irony of his situation! I chuckled and concluded there is no fairness when it comes to health or politics!]

17

"Political Physicians?"

Wednesday, January 16, 2018

What can't be disputed when it comes to something associated with the name TRUMP? A case in point, after the hour long grilling by non-medical reporters in the daily White House briefing, **The New York Times** reporter Michael D. Shear contacted a physician who was willing to challenge the integrity of the White House physician.

In an article published under the headline **"Trump's Physical Revealed Serious Heart Concerns, Outside Experts Say."** The article reports that Dr. Eric Topoi, a cardiologist at the Scripps Research Institute, "disputes the rosy assessment."

Yes, you read it correct. At least one cardiologist without ever examining President Trump gives his diagnosis: *"I would never use the word excellent health. How could take these indices and say excellent health? That is completely contradicted."*

Dr. Sanjay Gupta, the chief medical correspondent for CHH, repeatedly expressed concern on Wednesday about test results that showed Mr. Trump's coronary calcium score had increased to 133 from 34 in 2009. On CHH, Dr. Gupta repeatedly showed a chart suggesting that levels above 100 indicate someone with heart disease.

Unfortunately, this is a case of politicizing the integrity of the White House physician, Dr. Jackson. The good news, however, is that even the reporter posting this story included in his article the other side of the story by saying several former members of Mr. Obama's White House staff echoed praise for Dr. Jackson's assessment. The article ends with the comment:

"David Axelrod, who served as one of Mr. Obama's top advisors in the White House, said on Twitter Tuesday: "I knew Dr. Ronny Jackson in the White House. In my experience, he was very good guy and straight shooter."

What accountability is there for a physician to without examining a patient render a conclusion that contradicts a physician who examines and is in daily contact with the patient?

Shame on the physician who renders a "professional opinion" without examining a patient. Dr. Jackson has every reason to be offended—but one can only hope he suffers the challenge in silence and doesn't get into a political beef over the issue.

****

If there was concern the Dow Jones Index was only flirting with breaking the 26,000 mark the previous day, the Dow jumped 322 points to a record high at closing today at 26,115.

****

Donald Trump playfully announced his "Fake News" Awards on the internet and the interest was so great the volume crashed the website!

The number one award was given to Paul Krugman, the Nobel Prize winning economist for his prediction that if Trump were elected, there would be an unrecoverable decline in the stock market. Krugman did respond to the award by saying he let his emotional personal views get in the way of his economic judgment.

Other Award winners included the infamous report of the broadcaster who erroneously reported a Flynn story that dropped the Dow Jones Industrial Averages by almost 400 points until it was retracted, and the reporter lost his job.

Overall the Awards were given to 11 stories published since Trump took office. The awards were given to reporters who erroneously reported that Trump removed a bust of Martin Luther King, Jr. from the Oval Office after the election.

Another Award was given to the reporter who erroneously used a photo to misrepresent the size of a Trump rally. The photo was taken of a half-filled stadium an hour before the rally began. In truth, the rally was one in which Trump packed the stadium with supporters. When the awards the public interest was so great that the volume crashed the website!

The awards were a playful way Trump could scold the biased press with inaccurate and slanted news stories. It is highly unlikely the Awards will be viewed as a stigma—but will be worn as a badge of honor by Journalists who abhor Trump's Presidency.

18

"Betting Odds on 2020 Democratic Candidate"

Thursday, January 18, 2018

Forget about the political pollster predictions about 2020 election. It's time to depart from the political grief surrounding Washington politics and "follow the money." In other words, look at today's current betting odds with the Las Vegas gambler crowd if you want insight into who will be the Democratic candidate in 2020 Presidential race.

Here's a peak at how the gamblers are wagering today on the likely Democratic candidates. The most popular bets and the accompanying odds are as follows:

- Kamala Harris (6-1)
- Elizabeth Warren (7-1)
- Bernie Sanders (10-1)
- Hillary Clinton (25-1)
- Kirsten Gillibrand (10-1)

Let's see how the odds change by the end of the month of January.

If someone wants to get out of the most popular bet category, here is a more complete list and the odds:
- Joe Biden (10-1)
- Corey Booker (20-1)
- Michelle Obama (25-1)
- Andrew Cuomo (33-1)
- Al Gore (33-1)
- Tim Kayne (50-1)
- Jerry Brown (66-1)
- Chelsea Clinton (125-1)

* * * * * * *

The President appeared like he didn't want to gamble on the upcoming special election in Pennsylvania. He was on the campaign trail, in a sense, today as he traveled to the city of Coraopolis, Pennsylvania to meet with the HK Equipment Factory workers.

Ostensive, his speech purpose was to speak to a sympathetic audience about all the virtues of the tax reform bill and how it is helping the American people. In the speech he exclaimed the impact has been greater than even he anticipated.

His secondary and perhaps primary purpose was to support a Republican House candidate—Rick Saccone—who is vying for a vacated seat in a special mid-term election in March to replace Tim Murphy who represented the 18th congressional district until he was forced to resign after an embarrassing scandal. It is anticipated the Republican will prevail, but Trump is taking no chances.

During the speech Trump did deviated from his prepared remarks by commenting he thinks the Democrats want to cause a government shutdown as a diversion away from the extraordinary success of the tax reform bill that not a single Democrat supported in either house of Congress.

Back in Washington, the GOP expects to get House passage of the proposed bill, but pundits think there is a 50-50 chance it will stall in the Senate where the Democrats are digging in and preparing to blame the Republicans for the shutdown. The sticking point is Democratic demand for a solution to the DACA issue. The Republicans has included a six-year continuation of funding for the CHIP health care plan for children of families who have low income. Such a strategy is view by some critics as a way of making Democrats look bad if they vote down the proposed bill that gives much needed continuation of the CHIP legislation.

Both parties seem willing to try and shift the blame to the other if there is a government shutdown.

* * * * * * * * *

The comments CNN medical expert commentator, Dr. Sanjay Gupta, got a lot of flak from other medical experts for the diagnosis he made in which he asserted President Trump was suffering from Heart Disease.

The criticism of Gupta was generally based on how he was being unprofessional for making a diagnosis without examining a patient. Furthermore, Gupta is a neurosurgeon, not a cardiologist. He ignored the fact the White House physician—Dr. Ronny Jackson was a certified ER physician who performed a treadmill test on Trump, as well as an EKG, and other tests that led to his conclusion Trump was fit for duty and did not have heart disease. Several other physicians were critical of Dr. Gupta for implying Dr. Jackson was a medical hack.

One critic even went so far as to call Gupta *"a paid medical whore"* for selling a medical opinion to a hostile news media for political purposes. He clarified that "heart disease" is evidenced when during normal physical exercise the cardiovascular system shows signs and symptoms of stress such as chest pains and shortness of breath.

19

"Showdown on Shutdown!"

Friday, January 19, 2018

Welcome to the D.C. Swamp "Blame Game."

If one reads the Washington D.C. political "tea leaves" correctly the decision this morning for President Trump to post-pone his trip to Mar-a-Lago augers Trump's expectation a government shutdown is imminent.

Even though the House passed a budget bill and forward it to the Senate with a 230-197 favorable vote, Trump's behavior suggests he lacks confidence a deal will be reached so he is cancelling a $100,000 per ticket fundraising event designed to celebrate the one-year anniversary of his inauguration.

Midnight today the federal government runs us of money to fund our government. On Thursday night, the Senate adjourned without taking any vote on the House-passed funding bill.

Senate Majority Leader Mitch McConnell appears to be positioning the Senate to play a game of chicken on closing the government. Conversely, Senate Minority Leader, Chuck Schumer wanted to have a quick procedural vote to advance the Bill for a final vote, so his colleagues could kill the bill and begin new negotiations.

McConnell wants to put additional pressure on Democratic Senators facing tough re-election contests. He knows these vulnerable senators don't want to have to campaign in States where Trump won heavily and defend the position that they voted to shut down the government.

In an interview with **Fox News**, House Speaker Paul Ryan made it clear what he felt was happening in the Senate:

"These Senate Democrats are holding our men and women in uniform hostage over an unrelated issue. The Senate Democrat are holding children's health care hostage for an unrelated issue. . .They're basically holding all government hostage."

To find some ground for a "deal" President Trump invited Chuck Schumer to the White House this afternoon to discuss the situation. They had a discussion over a lunch of cheeseburgers and covered a wide range of issues. After the meeting

Schumer told the press he and Trump had a lengthy discussion and they made "some progress" but had no deal.

Up until the late-night hours, Democrats and Republicans scrambled to position themselves to cast their opponents into the role of shutdown causer. It wasn't until after the midnight deadline that Senate Majority Leader Mitch McConnell announced there was no deal. He told the Senate:

A government shutdown was 100 percent avoidable. Completely avoidable. Now it is imminent. Perhaps across the aisle some of our Democratic colleagues are feeling proud of themselves, but what has their filibuster accomplished. The answer is simple: Their very own government shutdown."

Following McConnell's speech, Senate Minority Leader Chuck Schumer chastised the Republicans and set the blame of Trump for the shutdown. He told the Senators:

"I reluctantly put the border wall on the table for discussion—even that was not enough to entice the president to finish the deal. What has transpired since that meeting in the Oval Office is indicative of the entire tumultuous and chaotic process Republicans have engaged in the negotiations thus far. Even though President Trump seemed to like

an outline of a deal in the room, he did not press his party in Congress to accept it."

The White House issued a statement through Press Secretary Sarah Huckabee Sanders reflecting the President's hard line position on further negotiations:

"We will not negotiate the status of unlawful immigrants while Democrats hold our lawful citizens hostage over their reckless demands. This is the behavior of obstructionist losers, not legislators. When Democrats start paying our armed forces and first responders we will reopen negotiations on immigration reform."

To respond to any Senate approved amendments to the failed House bill vote, the House Rules Committee met on Saturday morning to enact a provision to consider any Senate approved bill immediately. So, if the Senate approved a new short term bill the House can act immediately and re-open the government in a few hours.

Trump turned to his Twitter account and tweeted:

"The Democrats are holding our Military hostage over their desire to have unchecked illegal immigration. Can't let that happen"

20

"A Postponed Party"

Saturday, January 20, 2018

Today marks the anniversary of President Trump's first full year in office. It could have been a day of celebration at his estate in Mar-a-Lago capped by a festive fundraising party. Instead, a politically charged, divisive government shut-down has sent Congress into weekend negotiations to fix the blame-game stalemate.

Dan Mahaffee—Senior Vice President and Director of Policy at the Center for the Study of the Presidency and Congress in Washington D.C.—published an editorial in **The Hill** in which he argued that "Historic dysfunction in American Politics defines Trump Presidency."

His opening statement sets the theme of his editorial opinion:

"Looking back at President Trump's first year, it is almost telling that it ended with the specter of a

government shutdown. It reflects the continuing breakdown of political functioning yet provides the media the drama they need to remain in high dudgeon. . . . using the lens of history to understand the first year of the Trump presidency shows us how it is both a symptom of an accelerant to the breakdown in American politics."

Mahaffee concludes his well-written critique of the historic erosion of American politics by cynically observing: *"Washington will remain as partisan as ever, even as the economy continues to grow and the American people feel optimistic. What will perhaps define the second year of President Trump is whether the other institutions of the American economy and society can endure the division in our politics."*

* * * * * * *

After a daylong meeting that lasted into late Saturday night conferences, the Senate adjourned without finding any short term-solution to the budget bill impasse that has shut down the federal government.

This chapter is short and sweet. Whether we like it or not our partisan politics is eroding the ability of our government to govern!

21

"Sunday Stalemate"

Sunday, January 21, 2018

It is unfortunate the Senate can't rally, like the New England Patriots team under the leadership of quarterback Tom Brady and create a come-from-behind victory for the American People and end the budget impasse.

Congratulation for the impressive win—maybe before the Minnesota Vikings and the Philadelphia Eagle games ends tonight the two bickering political parties can settle on a compromise that will allow the U.S. Government to open for business after this nonsensical budget stalemate.

Early on Sunday morning President Trump tweeted:

Great to see how hard Republicans are fighting for our Military and Safety at the Border. The Dems just want illegal immigrants to pour into our nation unchecked.

Even though Senate Majority Leader Mitch McConnell disagrees with the President's solution of getting rid of the 60-vote filibuster rule that would allow the Republican majority vote to carry the day with a simple majority, McConnell did side with the president's view in a message he sent to the Senate:

"Bipartisan, bicameral negotiations have been underway for months. But they can go nowhere until Senate Democrats realize that the extreme path their leader has charted heads them nowhere."

Later in the afternoon, McConnell told the Senate: *"This shutdown is gonna get a lot worse tomorrow. Today would be a good day to end it."*

Well, we all know the fate of the bill! The Demos blinked and the "Schumer Shutdown became a blink in American political history!

22

"The Dysfunctional Washington Bridge Game!"

Monday, January 22, 2018

How do you trump Trump? Is he really the deal-maker? Or, doesn't he have a clue on how to play the Dysfunctional Washington Bridge Game?

Interim spending bill approved until Feb. 8. *"It's the economy stupid"* tax relief theme refocused. And, oh yes, it is also the "new normal" for the dysfunctional Congressional swamp-creatures. The bill passed the Senate 81-18. When it was forwarded to the House it passed 266-150. It was expected the President would sign the legislation late this evening. On Wednesday he is scheduled to fly to Darvo, Switzerland for the annual World Economic Forum meeting of the world's wealthiest businessmen.

The Dow Jones industrial average rose over 140 points as Wall Street once again yawned at the activities of Congress and continued its bullish market to new record numbers!

What President Trump labelled *"The Schumer Shutdown"* ended after 60 hours. An 81-18 favorable vote reopened the government. As hard as it was for Senate Minority Leader Schumer to admit he overplayed his hand. Trump played the trump-card and won this round of the Washington Dysfunctional Bridge Game.

Trump didn't blink—and after some late-night assessments of popularity polls, Senate Minority Leader Chuck Schumer capitulate on his hardline position of the "DACA immigration demand" and accepted essentially the same conditions he rejected to initiate his government shutdown Friday evening. The *"Schumer surrender"* as it was called by liberal democrats and immigration activists.

The outspoken, potential candidate for the Democratic nomination in 2020, Senator Kamala D. Harris voted no on the bill, telling her fellow Senators:

"I believe it's been a false choice that's been presented between keeping the government open

and resolving the DACA issue. I believe we can do both!"

There were several other Democratic Presidential hopefuls who voted against the bill, including Senator Bernie Sanders, Kirsten Gillibrand, and Elizabeth Warren.

While both sides gave a positive spin to the agreement and chose to claim victory, it appears there was a consensus of the pundits that President Trump had a short-term victory in causing Schumer and the Democrats to accept the terms of the bill.

The Republican majority leader, Mitchell McConnell gave a promise to the Senators that he would indeed introduce a clean bill to address the demands of the DACA advocate and that it would be on the floor before the February 8th deadline for such a vote.

It was pointed out by democrat critics of the bill that all they got for holding out, however, was they had to accept essentially the same terms rejected on Friday. McConnell only added his promise he would get an acceptable bill on DACA to the Senate floor—but not a promise it would pass.

Other critics who advocated the belief the Senate would indeed pass a bi-partisan bill were not so sure such a bill would pass muster when it went over to the House of Representatives.

McConnell's promise was ambiguous. *"This immigration debate will have a level playing field at the onset and an amendment process that is fair to all sides."*

The Democratic outrage over Schumer's capitulation was best characterized by one top liberal political strategists who was quoted in a **Washington Post** article written by Robert Costa:

"We're pissed off. We're not naïve to the politics. But give me a f---g break. They do something heroic Friday night they climb down Monday morning."

Senate Minority leader Schumer did his best to save face by telling his constituents in the Senate:

"I expect the majority leader to fulfill his commitment to the Senate, to me and to the bipartisan group, and abide by this agreement. If he does not. . .he will have breached the trust of not only the Democratic senators, but members of his own party as well."

Who were the winners and losers in the shutdown showdown? It appears the Congressional Republicans were winners as they held the ground and the Democrats compromised more to reopen the government.

The Republicans maintained and preserved for future negotiations in the few days leading up to a potential new shutdown threat. The Democrats only got a "promise" from the Republican leadership to bring forward a DACA bill—something they virtually had before the vote for the shutdown occurred.

So, the new normal appears to be to kick the can down the road. Set short-time spending limitations. Jockey to find a compromise position that will truly address immigration, so legislators can get on with the business of running the government on something other than a monthly funding budget crisis.

President Trump couldn't resist taking to his social media account to relish the victory over the Democrats in the Schumer Shutdown Showdown. He wrote several tweets after he signed the bill re-opening and funding the government at least through February 8th:

[Referring to an article by Jim Acosta that said Trump was *"dancing in the end zone"* and that *"Schumer and Demos caved,"* and *"the opposition party gambled and lost."* Trump wrote:

"Even crazy Jim Acosta of Fake News CNN agrees. "Trump World and WH sources dancing in end zone. Trump wins again. Schumer and Dems caved, gambled and lost." Thank you for your honesty, Jim."

Trump later added to his victory boast by tweeting optimism about finding a permanent solution to the budget and the immigration impasse:

"Big win for Republicans as Democrats cave on Shutdown. Now I want a big win for everyone, including Republicans, Democrats and DACA, but especially for our Great Military and Border Security. Should be able to get there. See you at the negotiating table."

23

"A Secret Society?"

Tuesday, January 23, 2018

Why not up the ante and modify the political-speak of the Trump-era of politics. Stop talking about an anti-Trump *"deep state!"* Make it more colorful by substituting the name *"Secret Society!"*

That is precisely what the mainstream media introduced into the anti-Trump political rhetoric.

Recall how after the time President Obama left office there was suspicion by right-wing conspiracy theorists that Obama loyalists who remained in government positions formed an unofficial alliance to undermine the activities of the incoming Trump administration. Such a suspicion was only levied at career government employees wishing to stay in their roles and at the same time not be supportive of the new administration. The conservative, right-wing media referred to this reality as "the deep state."

It wasn't until the emergence of information about two FBI agents having a romantic affair intermingled with their anti-Trump rhetoric that suspicions arose about anti-Trump sentiments infecting the otherwise apolitical activities of the FBI and some of its top-ranking officials.

In an article published by Olivia Beavers for **The Hill** under the headline *"GOP lawmakers raise concerns over 'secret society' in the FBI texts,"* the reporter cites comments made on **FOX NEWS** to Martha MacCallum.

The new, improved rhetoric of conspiracy-theory was used by Congressman Trey Gowdy. It was made about comments exchanged between the now infamous couple of FBI employees—Peter Strzok and his mistress FBI attorney Lisa Page.

Trey Gowdy is a member of the House Judiciary Committee. He has seen what is purported to be a "damming" four-page memo in which there is supposed evidence pointing to corruption among high ranking FBI and Department of Justice officials.

Supposedly the memo adds credence to those who argue the Obama administration used dubious and unverified evidence to convince a FISA Judge to warrant surveillance of President-elect Trump and his transition team. Trey Gowdy and fellow committee member John Radcliffe both appeared on Martha MacCallum **FOX NEWS** show. The two congressmen are heading a campaign to release the damming memo to the public. The two men told MacCallum:

"We learned today about information that in the immediate aftermath of his election, there may have been a 'secret society' of folks within the Department of Justice and the FBI, to include Page and Strzok, working against him. I'm not saying that actually happened, but when folks speak in those terms, they need to come forward to explain the context," Ratcliff told MacCallum.

Several of the House representatives who have read the four-page memo express disgust and outrage at its contents—claiming if the facts are true it, opens a scandal that dwarfs the Watergate scandal of the Nixon administration.

Supposedly, Page and Strzok sent over 50,000 e-mail messages to each other during the post-election transition period. What complicates the investigation of the alleged "secret society" is the discovery that the FBI coincidentally "lost" roughly a five-month span of e-mails.   This unexplained number of missing messages leads conspiracy-theorists to fuel claims such a society does in fact exist.

Once the four-page memo is made public it will lead to further outcries that the Robert Muller special investigation of Russian Collaboration with the Trump administration was initiated as a part of an anti-Trump "insurance plan" [as it was referred to in e-mails between Page and Strzok].

The talk of FBI and Justice Department corruption has caused Attorney General Jeff Sessions to get involved in the matter.   Sessions announced on Monday, Jan. 22nd:

"We will leave no stone unturned to confirm with certainty why these text message are not now available to be produced and will use every technology available to determine whether the missing messages are recoverable from another source."

If there is, indeed, corruption among some of the top FBI and Justice Department leaders, then President Trump will be vindicated for his hasty conclusion that the Muller investigation has been in fact "a witch hunt."

* * * * * * * *

Perhaps because he is still smarting from all the grief his fellow Democrats gave him for caving in on the shutdown before getting a DACA deal, Senate Minority Leader Chuck Schumer has rescinded his offer to agree to funds for the border wall.

Allegedly, Schumer agreed to support Trump's efforts to fund the wall up to a $25 million-dollar number. The Trump administration indicated that if Schumer's offer was being withdrawn as negotiations now move forward on a DACA solution it would be a step backwards.

Schumer appears to have read Trump's book **The Art of the Deal** and is looking at strategies that don't encumber him with former offers when new negotiations occur.

24

"NO WALL, NO DACA"

Wednesday, January 24, 2018

Last Night, President Trump delivered an unequivocal message to Charles Schumer regarding the issue the Senate Minority Leader used in his unsuccessful bit to leverage a Government Shutdown to get a DACA bill through Congress.

Because of getting a lot of heat for caving in on the DACA negotiations to avoid prolonging the government shutdown, Schumer went on record with reporters with this message:

"We're going to have to start on a new basis and the wall offer is off the table."

In response to hearing Schumer has now taken funds for a Wall off the negotiating table, Trump sent out this Twitter:

"Cryin' Chuck Schumer fully understands, especially after his humiliating defeat, that if there is no Wall, there is no DACA. We must have safety and security, together with a strong Military, for our great people!"

One must wonder if the moderates in both political parties who want a DACA deal—as does 75% of the Americans polled—can somehow prevail and get a Bill past the Senate and the House before the Feb. 8 deadline? If they don't, what are the chances of another shutdown, or, even sadder, another short term continuing resolution to avoid a shutdown?

* * * * * * * *

President had a lot of support for the economic message he delivered to a gathering of U.S. Mayors held at the White House today. It could be viewed as his rehearsal for the message he is carrying to the World Economic Forum where he is scheduled to travel tonight to Darvo, Switzerland.

The Stock Market Dow Jones Average ended today's trading session with a record high of

26,252—a 41.21 increase in the index over the previous trading day.

Despite his enthusiastic boasting of America's thriving economy, the meeting was tarnished by several Mayors—mostly Democrats—boycotting the meeting to protest the recent ruling of the Department of Justice to begin putting economic pressure on cities that declare they are "sanctuary cities" and unwilling to assist federal ICE agents seeking cooperation to hold and deport illegal immigrants who commit crimes.

The group of members in a bipartisan U.S. Conference of Mayors are holding their annual winter meeting in Washington D.C. As a part of the meeting the Mayors were invited to the White House to talk with President Trump.

Unfortunately, the head of the group, Mitch Landrieu, Mayor of New Orleans—an aspiring Presidential hopeful—told the press that some members were boycotting the meeting. He told the press:

"Many mayors of both parties were looking forward to visiting the White House. Unfortunately, the Trump administration's decision to threaten mayors and demonize immigrants yet again—and use cities ad political

props in the process—has made this meeting untenable."

New York Mayor, Bill de Blasio, was leading the boycott and told the press he and several others were not attending *"Because Donald Trump's Department of Justice decided to renew their racist assault on our immigrant communities."*

Other prominent democrats who also boycotted the meeting included Chicago's Rahm Emanuel and Eric Garcetti of Los Angeles.

Undaunted by the absence of some Mayors, President Trump went ahead and hosted the meeting at the White House. He used the occasion to criticize "sanctuary city" mayors.

He told the audience in attendance:

"The mayors who choose to boycott this event have put the needs of criminal, illegal immigrants over law-abiding America. So, let me tell you the vast majority of people showed up."

After welcoming those in attendance, he proceeded to enumerate all the glowing economic statistics that have become the "America First, but Not Alone" message he will be carrying to the World Economic Forum.

Trump told the Mayors he is attending the meeting in Switzerland to invite world economic leaders and international business corporate CEOs that America's cities are open for business and would welcome all companies to expand their business ties with America.

25

"Scratch Oprah from Candidate List"

Thursday, January 25, 2018

The beloved TV personality Oprah Winfrey's potential presidential candidacy proved to be a shooting-star other than a Democratic "rising star."

The Vegas odds-makers can take the popular media mogul Oprah Winfrey off the list of aspiring Democratic hopefuls for the 2020 Presidential candidates—at least for the time being.

Even though her longtime partner Stedman Graham earlier this month told a reporter from the Los Angeles Times that Oprah was indeed considering a run, she recently formally dismissed such speculation.

In an interview with **InStyle** Magazine published today she told the reporter she was not interested in making a presidential run. According to a story released by Reuters, she told the reporter:

"It's not something that interests me. . I met with someone the other day who said that they would help me with a campaign. That's not for me."

After much ado was made following Oprah's eloquent speech at the Golden Globes award ceremony, Donald Trump acknowledged Oprah was a friend and he held her in high esteem. He also boasted he would welcome such a challenge because he would beat her in an election.

* * * * * * * *

Today, however, President Trump's mind and person were far away from thoughts of his 2020 election challenger. This morning Air Force One landed in Darvo, Switzerland and Trump prepared to rub shoulders with wealthy business leaders from around the world at the World Economic Forum.

Trump's goal when he speaks to the conference tomorrow is to tell the story of the remarkable revival of the American economy and to invite major international companies to do more business in America—to add physical plants and hire more American workers. He has modified his *"America*

First" message with the words *"America First, but not Alone!"*

It is no secret Trump's anti-global perspective and his criticism of international trade deals that in the past have been unfavorable toward America have alienated several world leaders. And, his most recent alleged comment about African "shit-hole countries, have alienated many.

In fact, a prominent African business organization, known as Business Leadership South Africa, is said to be planning a walk-out of the conference when Trump addresses the meeting. Trump is scheduled to meet with Rwandan president Kagame, who is the chairman of the African Union. The purpose of the meeting is for Trump to reaffirm U.S. relationship with Africa and to discuss shared priorities.

On the home front, Congressional leaders in the House continue to pursue release of the four-page memo that allegedly cast aspersions on the top leadership of the FBI and the DOJ. The DOJ leadership has not yet seen the allegedly damaging memo, but Democratic leadership is encouraging the House Judiciary Committee Chair Nunez to not note to release the document because it could jeopardize national security and expose sources otherwise guarded by the intelligence community.

The contention of right-wing critics is that the document demonstrates some in the intelligence community have "weaponized" their roles to undermine the Presidency.

Related to the FBI and DOJ scandal emerging related to the e-mail exchanges between agents Page and Strzok. The mysterious disappearance of five months of text messages apparently have been recovered by a DOJ internal watchdog function and will be shared with congressional committees.

26

"Trump In Darvo"

Friday, January 26, 2018

A picture is worth a thousand words—like pictures of crowded tarmacs at the airports in Zurich, Milan, Austria, and other surrounding countries that traffic visitors to the World Economic Forum's meeting at the exclusive ski resort and conference center in Darvo, Switzerland.

The crowd of prestigious billionaires who self-righteously clamor for international agreements to curb global warming seem to capriciously ignore their own contribution to the carbon footprint they view as one of the culprit of global warming.

A cynic could scoff at the massive aircraft known as Air Force One taxied to a spot on one of the crowded tarmacs. The image illustrated how the arrival of President Donald Trump was as out of place at the liberal bastion of globalists as the glut of gas guzzling jets were at the several international airports surrounding Darvo. There was no denying Trump's ride was the largest and most conspicuous. Unlike his globalists counterparts, such an ostentatious display of political incorrect consumption and contribution to the dreaded "carbon footprint" fit the Forum's image of the nationalist Donald Trump.

Several journalists following the Trump visit to the World Economic Forum commented that, like or dislike Trump, attendees were falling all over themselves to get selfies with Trump and to rub shoulders with the controversial American president.

It was pleasing to see **CNN** journalists Alanna Petroff and Ivana Kottasova were generally objective in their reporting of Trump visit to Darvo. They wrote:

"How did Darvos respond to President Trump's much-anticipated speech? The American president was by far the hottest ticket at the World Economic Forum. . Attendees flocked to see the speech, which began with a musical performance and warm greeting from organizer Klaus Schwab. Trump spoke to aa packed conference hall on Friday, and more attendees watched on screens in three overflowing rooms."

In his whirl-wind trip to the conference he met with several U.S. allied nations before giving one of the keynote speeches at the conference.

Trump's message was outlined in an **Associated Press** article written by Jonathan Lemire. He wrote:

"Trump told the World Economic Forum in Davos, an incongruous location for a nationalist president, that American prosperity has created countless jobs around the world, but stress that his priority would always remain on protecting the interests within his national's own borders."

Lemire's article said some in the audience hissed and booed when Trump was introduced. For the most part, the audience was polite as they listened to Trump's well-worn "America First" political spiel now modified to include the trailer "But not Alone."

The only overt negative reaction was when Trump *"took a swipe at how nasty, how mean, how vicious and how fake the press can be."*

* * * * * * * *

If U.N. Ambassador Nickki Haley had been present at the conference, she would have risen and objected to the audience's reaction to Trump's claim. After, all on the very day Trump gave his speech and uttered the fake news comment, she was the victim of a vicious false rumor spread by the author of the controversial book **Fire and Fury**. Haley made her comments in an interview published in **Politico.**

In an interview with HBO's Bill Maher, Michael Wolff made the innuendo slur against Trump and Haley. Wolff told Maher he was "absolutely sure" the President was having an affair. He told Maher they could put the pieces together after they read a certain paragraph in his book. The paragraph reads:

"The president has been spending a notable amount of private time with Haley on Air Force One and was seen to be grooming her for a national political future."

Lemire's article indicates Haley was "highly offended" and "disgusted."

When the **Politico** folks contacted Wolff for comment he didn't reply.

And, as a footnote to the continuing positive impact Trump's administration is having on the economic front, the Dow Jones continued its upward movement, again closing at an all-time high of over a 220-point gain!

The strong economic performance on the home front appeared to underscore Trump's Darvo theme that *"America is open for business."* And its prospering is good for the world's economy.

27

"Feel the Bern?"

Saturday, January 27, 2018

The Democratic 2020 candidate stew is starting to bubble. Rumors started circulating that Former Presidential candidate defeated by George W. Bush, Former Secretary of State, John Kerry is testing the waters for another presidential run—this time against incumbent Donald Trump.

More curious, however, is the speculation that Senator Bernie Sanders is testing interest in those willing to back him for a second run.

Although he would be the oldest candidate to run for President, according to an article written by Rachel Wolfe for **Vox,** Sanders is serious about another run. Wolfe wrote:

"Those hoping for another chance to 'Feel the Bern' in 2020 could have good reason to be optimistic about Bernie Sander's odds of running for the presidency."

Wolf reported that on Saturday, January 20, 2018, Sanders met with his top political advisers to discuss the possibility.

According to data obtained by Wolfe, Sanders is considered the most popular politician in America. He is also the most in-demand public speaker among "Democrats" and is the most prolific grassroots fundraiser in American history. She also points out that in some recent polls Sanders is currently beating Donald Trump.

What are the Vegas odds to place a bet on Bernie Sanders? After the speculation published today Sanders is a 20/1 bet. Trump is a 5/2 bet and Elizabeth Warren and Kamal Harris are both 14/1 bets.

* * * * * * * *

Enough said about this curious blink of Democratic politics. Is the party going to rekindle the warmth of the Bernie appeal to its younger constituency—a group that often reflects in polls they favor socialism over capitalism? Is the party going to agree it is once again "time to feel the Bern?"

28

"Draining the Swamp, Really?"

Sunday, January 28, 2018

Did somebody forget to tell the Washington D.C. lobbyist that President Trump intends to "drain the swamp?" Given the statistic compiled by Fredreka Schouten in an article for **USA Today**, such appears to be the case.

In her article published under the headline *"Draining the Swamp? D.C. lobbying during Trump administration surges to highest level in 7 years."*

According to data from the Center for Responsive Politics in 2017 there were 11,444 lobbyists registered to operate in Washington D.C.

The financial number is staggering. Schouten reports the lobbying activity was at its highest level since 2010—soaring to a whopping $3.34 billion dollars last year. By comparison, in 1998

$1/45 billion was spent on lobbying. In 2008 $3.50 billion was spent.

The Schouten article said its new data also came from *"The nonpartisan Center for Responsive Politics."*

The **USA Today** article concluded that the U.S. Chamber of Commerce and the National Association of Realtors spent the most money to shape policy in 2017.

One of the highest levels was the $18 million Google spent lobbying for relief from increased scrutiny and efforts to regulate online advertising.

Another major lobbyist effort was on behalf of the National Association of Realtors. It spent $22.2 million alone in the fourth-quarter of 2017— double what it spent the previous three months, according to congressional records. The efforts were aimed at influencing the real estate tax issue in the tax Reform bill eventually signed by President Trump.

The nonprofit Open Society Policy Center— funded heavily by George Soros--spent $16.1 million funded lobbying for such efforts linked to dealing with child trafficking and efforts to support Democratic congressional efforts to prohibit

Trump from making a preemptive strike against North Korea without Congressional approval.

* * * * * * *

The only way Trump is going to drain the swamp of so many lobbyists is, as suggested previously in this manuscript, is to limit terms of Congress elected officials in the House and Senate to a single-term with no needs to raise cash to run for a second term. Such a policy, in addition to other rules that would preclude elected officials from receiving money or other post-Congress gratuities and considerations, would go a long way toward eliminating corruption in our government system.

29

"Disclosing the 'Secret Memo'"

Monday, January 29, 2018

For the past several weeks a so-called "damming memo" written by the House Intelligence Committee has circulated among members of the House. The 'Nunes memo' as it is called after the name of Representative Nunes, a Republican from California who serves as chair of the committee, alleges it identifies "shocking surveillance abuses' by the DOJ and FBI top officials in the Obama administration.

Even though the Nunes committee voted last week to allow all Congressmen to read the summary memo, its content remains undisclosed to the Senate, the Justice Department, and the public—as well as the White House.

It is expected that today the Committee will vote to make the document public. If that occurs in the meeting today, the memo will go to the Trump White House. If Trump objects to making it public, then the full House would vote on the matter. Trump can also approve it immediately. If he does nothing, it will be released in five days.

Democrat who have read the memo contend it is not controversial and has as its main purpose to derail the Muller investigation. They also contend it is not a report on an investigation and it contains information about irregularities related to the securing of a FISA decision that contains speculation that readers might construe as facts.

* * * * * * * *

The Nunes Memo appears to have rattled the its democratic opponents so much that a counter-argument memo has been drafted in an effort to pre-empt any alarming or condemning conclusion Nunes' memo might stir in the court of public opinion once it is made public.

If early claims about it naming names of top officials who are currently associated with Robert Muller's investigation are true, it might trigger serious talks about ending the Muller investigation.

30

"Trump's State of the Union Speech"

Tuesday, January 30, 2018

Like all the State of the Union addresses given before him, the first Trump speech was a long time in the making. And, days before the event, the media was filled with leaks and previews designed to foreshadow the theme of the speech.

In an article written by Jonathan Lemire and Zeke Miller of the **Associated Press,** the two journalists were given this preview they shared with readers:

"The theme of his Tuesday night address to Congress and the country is 'Building a safe, strong and proud America.'"

According to the **AP** article five themes are expected to dominate: the economy and tax overhaul, infrastructure, immigration, trade, and terrorism and global threats.

Apparently, drafts of the speech were written by White house policy advisor and staff secretary Rob Porter. Several drafts were circulated among staff in the West Wing and the President weighed in with hand-written notes.

Trump seemed anxious to kick off the prelude to his speech with some late-night tweets aimed at his democratic critics:

"I have offered DACA a wonderful deal, including a doubling in the number of recipients and a twelve-year pathway to citizenship, for two reasons: 1) because the Republicans want to fix a long-time terrible problem. 2) To show that Democrats do not want to solve DACA only use it"

In a later tweet he wrote:

"Democrats are not interested in Border Safety & Security or in the funding and rebuilding of the Military. They are only interested in obstruction!"

Such hostile and antagonistic tweets caused some critics to question whether this foreshadowed a more partisan posture in the upcoming speech.

One thing we know in advance, several Congress representatives are boycotting the event: Jayapal of Washington; Blumenauer, Oregon; John Lewis, Georgia; Jan Schakowsky, Illiniois; Albio Sires,

New Jersey; Maxine Waters, California, and Frederica Wilson, Florida.

In addition to the several Democratic Representatives, Supreme Court Justice Ruth Ginsburg will not attend because of a previously scheduled speaking engagement.

It now remains to be see how the event transpires, how Trump intones the message, and how critics evaluate the success of the event.

* * * * * * * *

The speech itself was too long—as are most of these institutional conventional messages. The President spoke for more than an hour and 20 minutes. Although the pre-press message from the White House was the speech was supposed to be one about unity, one only had to look at the reactions of the Democrats in the audience to see they seldom stood or applauded any of the accomplishments Trump touted in his speech.

Trump began his speech with the message of optimism for all American. He told the audience: *"This is, in fact, our new American moment. There has never been a better time to start living the American dream.!*

The critics and talking-head pundit who opined in media shows after the speech were complimentary of how Trump effectively wove the stories of many of the guests that were seated with his wife Melania. Each of the invited guests served as a way of introducing many of the themes and issues of Trump's address.

Perhaps the most noteworthy line of the speech was when Trump said: *"all Americans are 'dreamers.'* The President continued to return to the theme it was time to unify congress and work across the aisle to address immigration reform, infrastructure rebuilding, new reductions in restrictive government regulations, and significant reduction in cost of medical drugs as well as relaxing FDA control of experimental drugs for people looking for terminal disease management and miracle cures.

Trump was interrupted 115 times with applause from the GOP side of the audience—the loyal opposition remained silent and stoically when the spontaneously clapping started. Many were dressed in black and wearing colors of Mexico to symbolize support for Dreamers.

After the speech the media coverage switched to the Democratic response message. It was delivered by Joe Kennedy, III, the young representative from the State of Massachusetts. He delivered it in front of a small audience in a vocational tech school in Fall River, a rural town in Mass.

It was obvious the Democrats wanted to showcase one of its young, attractive, articulate rising stars. Kennedy gave a rousing speech that didn't rebut Trump speech as much as it used the same themes from a different perspective. His main theme was inclusiveness. He told the audience: *"Their record is a rebuke of our highest American ideal; the belief that we are all worthy, we are all equal and we all count."*

Kennedy said: *"Trump's economic policies are not a bridge to the future; it's a tunnel back to the Gilded Age."*

After painting a contrasting view to the President's optimism, Kennedy concluded: *"Ladies and gentlemen, have faith. The state of our union is hopeful, resilient, enduring."*

Even though Kennedy was the media showcased respondent to the Trump speech, several other Democrats used the occasion to give other formal responses. Elizabeth Warren, Bernie Sanders, and Nancy Pelosi all made formal statements. One pundit observed how the multiple spokepersons was a foreshadow of the lack of any singular leader or policy currently driving the Democratic party as it heads into the mid-term elections and begins the search for the 2020 candidate. Kennedy was certainly a refreshing glimpse of the youth movement among the democrats.

One of the **Fox News** pundits—Juan Williams—the democratic advocate—made what was one of the more candid view of the whole State of the Union event. He observed how symbolic it was that both parties seemed to look at the same set of facts and draw significantly different conclusions about "the State of the Union." His perspective reinforced how divided the country is as we launch the journey toward the mid-term elections.

31

"January In Retrospect"

Wednesday, January 31, 2018

Perhaps poet T.S. Eliot was wrong when he wrote in his epic poem **"The Waste Land"** that *"April is the cruelest month."*

If the many Trump-hating journalist have their way they would all like to craft February as the cruelest month for our current President Donald J. Trump. Many in the "resist Trump" movement awaken each morning determined to uncover something unsavory that will further bifurcate the two cultures of America and decrease voters' confidence in President Trump's fitness for office.

And, anyone who watches the on-going sparing match between Trump and what he calls "fake news" can see it is a punching match the President often appears to enjoy. He seems to delight in egging-on his media critics.

For better or worse, it is going to be a signature dimension of the Trump administration for the duration of the Trump-era—at least until a new Democratic leader emerges and takes charge of the loyal opposition party.

Trump's battle with the media exists because of two factors: 1) the media has become the surrogate voice of the opposing party that now lacks a physical persona for its true leader; and, 2) once the new Democratic leader surfaces, BOTH Trump and the media will re-focus. Trump will focus on the new Democratic leader; and, the media will spend time and column inches championing and writing about the new leader and less about Trump.

By the end of January, however, the Democratic Party is no closer to identifying a new rising-star to lead the party to a victory over incumbent Donald Trump in the 2020 presidential election. Internal conflict in the Democratic Party appears to be the effort of the party to move closer to the moderate center and away from the ultra-left leading tendencies of its establishment members.

It is likely the efforts of Special Investigator Robert Muller will come to a head—and finally put to rest its case against Trump on the grounds of a conspiracy theory; or, more likely, a charge of obstruction of justice. Against the backdrop of a Muller report, the GOP will make its own case charging abuse of power by some of the DOJ and FBI top executives during the Obama administration.

If the Muller case comes to a successful conclusion, [AKA make a cogent and defensible charge against Trump] it could certify February as the cruelest month!

But the February prelude to the 2018 mid-term elections is yet to be recorded. That will be the subject of the next book in this year-long epic history.

* * * * * * * *

When looking back at January from a historical perspective, however, this first month of 2018 might be characterized in political poetry praising the Trump administration as "January is the Jewel Month!

January saw the American economy beginning to realize the many benefits of Trump's Tax-Reform policy. The metrics of successes included:

- Highest stock market advances with the Dow ending the month at an all-time high above 26,000—an astounding climb from the 18,000 level when Trump took office
- Highest consumer confidence level since the metric was tracked decades ago
- Lowest unemployment rate in decades
- Highest number of employment among Afro-Americans and Hispanics
- Indicators that through corporate bonuses and wage increases there is indeed the extra benefit of corporate tax-relief trickling down to middle-class wage earners
- Significant evidence of corporations re-investing money in expanding American business and increasing jobs
- Etc. etc.

January saw Trump lay the groundwork for a new immigration policy. He put on the negotiating table for debate a comprehensive method for resolving the DACA issue and the complete immigration problem. His proposed plan limits the number of immigrants accepted each year through legitimate channels. It expands the number of eligible DACA eligible people from 800 thousand to 1.8 thousand people. It advocates ending the lottery system. It limits chain immigration to immediate families. It funds a wall-system on the Mexican border. And, it creates an immigration system based on merit and ability to enhance and contribute to the American economic growth.

If Trump's greatest legislative victory was the Tax-reform bill, then his second greatest achievement during this first month of the New Year was to remain firm on his position regarding the Wall. Indeed, after breaking the "Schumer Shutdown" Trump maintained his position with the declaration, *"No Wall, No DACA."*

It was also appropriate in ending the month of January, Trump took his modified America First policy to the international World Economic Forum in Davos. Trump reiterated his domestic policy of America First was good for the rest of the World. He argued it is not isolationism and protectionism, but patriotism and participation with other countries on a level playing field of reciprocal free-trade agreements.

Finally, in his first State of the Union Address to the Joint Session of Congress, Trump highlighted his first-year successes and pledged his continuing dedication to furthering his America First policy at home and abroad.

The Jewel month of January is history. It now remains to open the pages of February and see what twists and turns the "resist Trump" movement makes to swing the political pendulum in the direction of the Democratic Party.

Who will emerge as the new leader of the Democratic Party? Will it be someone from the old guard like Warren, Sanders, Biden, or even Kerry? Or will it be a newcomer like Harris or Booker?

Stay tuned. February might be a mixture of gloom and doom as well as continuing economic success for the Trump administration. It might also be a period of resurrection and reinvigoration for the Democratic opposition.

It will be good for our country when the Democratic party settles on its new leader and begins to seriously create the framework of policies that differ from the current administration.

Our country desperately needs a strong two- party system so we can maintain a healthy democracy.

At this moment in history there is nothing to compare or contrast. The battle seems to be between the incumbent President and his policies and the "resist-Trump" voice of the main-stream that is serving as the surrogate for the leader of a currently leaderless party.

The only image the public has is the wearisome personas of Nancy Pelosi and Chuck Schumer who are likewise forced to embody their party's old-guard leadership until the new person surfaces.

Will February get us any closer to learning which Democratic leader will play the cards that will finally "trump" Trump?

www.ingramcontent.com/pod-product-compliance
Lightning Source LLC
Chambersburg PA
CBHW070706250726
48662CB00001B/286